Collins *gem*

Psychic
Powers

Car

HarperCollins Publishers Ltd.
77–85 Fulham Palace Road
London
W6 8JB

www.collins.co.uk

Collins is a registered trademark of HarperCollins Publishers Ltd.

First published in 2007
Text © 2007 Carolyn Boyes
Illustrations © 2007 HarperCollins Publishers

13 12 11
7 6 5 4

A catalogue record for this book is available from the British Library.

ISBN-13: 978-0-00-724201-6

Designed by Martin Brown
Printed and bound in China

CONTENTS

INTRODUCTION

What do we mean by psychic powers?

Psychic powers are powers that cannot be explained by the laws of the physical Universe alone. These include extrasensory abilities, such as telepathy, clairvoyance and precognition, as well as applied powers that are beyond our current ability to explain, for example, astral projection, mediumship and telekinesis.

These kinds of powers are controversial. Many people doubt they even exist, and others devote time to proving they are the work of fraudsters and charlatans. However, equally, many people believe that there are such things as the paranormal and 'psi phenomena', psychic abilities, magic, and esoteric knowledge that we do not yet understand scientifically but can learn. According to metaphysics - a branch of philosophy that seeks to understand all aspects of the world - there is more to the Universe than we can detect through our normal five senses. This physical Universe is just part of a much bigger Universe.

About this book

Collins Gem Psychic Powers lays out the most common theories about the psychic cosmos. These are fundamental to developing any latent psychic talents of your own.

It is intended to be useful as a general reference and an explanation of the breadth and depth of the psychic powers you may come across.

The book is also a practical guide to developing psychic powers. It is structured so that you will have learnt the basics before you try out more advanced techniques. It explores different types of psychic ability: what they are and how you might develop them.

There are many different psychic talents. As with any skill, you may find that you have a particular aptitude for one ability rather than another. Some abilities take practice, others you are born with. Use the book to experiment with different techniques and discover your unique combination of talents.

HISTORY OF PSYCHIC POWERS

Throughout the history of mankind there have been those who claimed supernatural powers: the power to predict the future or to converse with the spirits. Early man was in no doubt that his ancestors were alive after death and still had powers that could affect the living, so he practised ancestor worship, including spirit communication.

Consulting the spirits was part of all the great early civilisations. The ancient Greeks, Chinese and Romans all practised divination and consulted oracles as a way of asking for spirit guidance, while mediumship also played an important part in early Christianity. But the Middle Ages put an end to open displays of mediumship in the Western world. In the fourth century, the Christian Council of Nicaea proclaimed that mediums and sorcerers were the servants of the Devil, and God's guidance should only be sought through priests. As a result, those who practiced the psychic arts were accused of being witches under the Pope's decree of 1484, and they were ordered to be put to death.

Spiritualism

In the 1800s in Europe and America a widespread interest in spirit communication came to the fore once more. The forerunners of the modern interest in psychic phenomena were two movements in the nineteenth century: Mesmerism and Spiritualism. Franz Anton Mesmer (1734–1815) was the inventor of Mesmerism, the forerunner of hypnosis (invented by James Braid, 1795–1860). He was the first person in the Victorian Age to formulate a theory about mind overruling matter. He showed that the power of suggestion could have an extraordinary effect on the body. His techniques awakened interest in America and Britain in the idea of non-physical powers. Famous British writers such as Charles Dickens, Charlotte Brontë and Elizabeth Barrett Browning were all interested in Mesmer's phenomena. Mesmerism became popular in Europe and America, but soon it was overtaken by a new fashion for contacting the dead, called Spiritualism.

Modern Spiritualism began in 1848 in America, when sisters Margaretta and Catherine Fox of Hydesville, New York State, established communication with a spirit who was responsible for noisy rapping sounds within the family home. The case garnered great publicity and brought the idea of spirit communication and mediumship into the open once again. By the middle of the century, the new Spiritualism movement had two million followers. In America, and in Britain (from 1852), home séances became popular, and many former followers of Mesmer became mediums.

Early on, Spiritualism mainly consisted of physical demonstrations of spirit communication, such as table-rapping and table-tilting or turning. Soon, other ways of proving spirit existence, such as spirit photography, became popular and many mediums took to the stage, taking Spiritualism to a public audience.

Research

Spiritualism was taken very seriously by a number of scientists in the nineteenth century. Several societies were set up to investigate aspects of Spiritualism. These included The British National Association of Spiritualists (1873) – now the College of Psychic Science – and the Society for Psychical Research (1882).

A key work of this time was *The Scientific Aspect of the Supernatural* in 1866, a scientific investigation of the alleged powers of clairvoyants and mediums, written by Alfred Russel Wallace, (1823–1913), whose work on the theory of evolution predated Darwin's. He was also a key proponent of the new spirit photography.

Another key figure was Sir Oliver Lodge (1851–1940), a British physicist who was the first man to transmit a radio signal. A committed Spiritualist and Christian, he was the president of the Society for Psychical Research. He investigated psychic phenomena with Sir Arthur Conan Doyle, the author of *A History of Spiritualism* (1926).

Occult groups

A number of occult groups were set up in the nineteenth century, some of which survive to this day. They were influenced by Spiritualism, Egyptian magic, medieval grimoires, the Tarot and Eastern mysticism. The cabbala (also spelt Kabbalah and Qabbalah), the ancient Jewish esoteric tradition, was a particular influence. It has roots that go back about 4,000 years and provides a model or cosmology of the invisible Universe as well as a guide to the rules of the Universe and methods for expanding personal esoteric consciousness.

The Hermetic Order of the Golden Dawn was set up in 1888 by Samuel Liddell MacGregor Mathers (1854–1918). The group claimed many influential members including W B Yeats, and became highly influential on the Western Mystery tradition. Notable among its adherents have been the occultists Aleister Crowley (1875–1947) and Dion Fortune (1891–1946).

THE PSYCHIC UNIVERSE

The geography of the Universe

The nature of the psychic cosmos is not so far provable by normal scientific means. However, there are remarkably similar traditions of theories about its nature that have been passed down in the world's secret and esoteric traditions, including Gnosticism, the Kabbalah, Sufism, Neo-Platonism, Tantra and Theosophy.

Most ancient philosophies hold that the Universe as a whole is greater than the physical Universe. The Universe was created by a mind or power, commonly referred to as God. The visible or physical Universe is only one part of a bigger Universe that is filled with different non-physical levels or planes, spheres or dimensions in which there are living energies.

Different traditions vary in their description of the details of the dimensions of the Universe. For example, Kabbalah's Tree of Life, which provides one of the most influential maps of the Universe, describes ten spheres or sephirot, each of which has a different quality of God within it. There are paths between each, and five worlds or trees in all. The lowest of these contains the physical world.

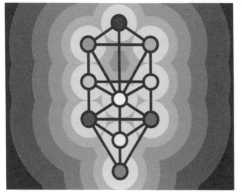

The Tree of Life

In the Victorian era, theosophy proposed the idea that there are seven planes and 49 subplanes within the cosmos. These planes are sometimes referred to as eggs. They interpenetrate each other, and at each level become denser and more embodied. In Hindu thinking, there are also seven lokas or worlds, and in Buddhist thinking, there are a number of deva lokas.

Throughout the many esoteric traditions, the Universe as a whole is generally thought to be without limits. It has no beginning and no end. This means that we may draw on a limitless resource as we learn how to access the other planes.

The elements

Western and Eastern cosmologies bear remarkable similarities in the elements that make up the fabric of the Universe. The Tattwas in Hindu cosmology describe five elements that mould space and interstellar dust into matter. Chinese cosmology, and the underlying theories of Chinese medicine, also has five elements: wood, fire, metal, water and earth. According to Western esoteric cosmology, which is

Chinese elements

based on Greek philosophy, the Universe is made up of four basic qualities – heat, humidity, cold, dryness – which produce the elements fire, water, earth and air. Fire comes from heat and dryness; water from cold and humidity; earth from cold and dryness; and air from heat and humidity.

Ether

In addition to the four elements of fire, water, earth and air, there is a fifth, ether. Ether (sometimes spelt aether) is the source of all intelligence in the Universe. Ether is the stuff that makes up the force field of the physical Universe. Within the invisible Universe, the equivalent force sustaining the other planes of existence is known as astral light.

Western elements

Ether is the life force that sustains all the molecules and atoms in the Universe. On the emotional plane, it is the force of pure love. The major esoteric systems throughout the world each describe this force, although they give it different names. Scientists, including Western alchemists, have tried to prove the existence of ether but have so far been unsuccessful.

Ether has its equivalents in all the great cultures that have attempted to describe the nature of the Universe:

Names for Ether	Tradition
Ch'i (Qi)	Chinese
Ki	Japanese
Fohat	Theurgist
Akasha	Hindu
I'o, Iao	Hawaiian
The Clear Light	Buddhist
Quintessence / The Fifth Element	Alchemist
Ether	Gnostic/Renaissance

The afterlife

The afterlife is contained within the non-physical dimensions of the Universe. When the physical body dies (or passes on), the soul or spirit still lives on in an afterlife on the higher planes (sometimes referred to as the other side, the hereafter or heaven).

Your soul or spirit is the essence of you that is interconnected with your physical body, but that is able to live beyond death. It has a permanent channel of communication open to the other planes. It is thought that our souls choose our physical life for our own development. In the afterlife, or 'other side', our soul goes through a transition that is part of our ongoing learning and evolution.

Extrasensory perception

While we sense the visible Universe through our sight, sounds, taste, touch, smell, the invisible Universe is outside the perception of these five senses. Nevertheless, the invisible Universe touches and affects our physical life at all times. We must use the non-physical senses, extrasensory perception (ESP), to perceive aspects of this vast, invisible Universe.

Scientists know that our material world is not static. Everything in the physical world that appears to be static is, in fact, made up of vibrating particles. The spirits who inhabit the higher dimensions of the Universe vibrate at higher frequencies that are faster than the speed of light. This is why we can only communicate with them through extrasensory means.

A medium can bridge the gap between the material and invisible Universes, and contact both intelligences or spirits that live permanently on the higher planes and those who have crossed over after life in the physical Universe. When the medium communicates with someone who has died, the spirit appears in a form that is recognisable to their relations and friends as the person they used to be on the earthly plane. However, just as someone grows older during his life on Earth, he is still evolving and developing on his new plane, although losing the physical limitations and weaknesses of an aging body.

In a reading with a medium, a spirit will often come through to communicate the lessons he has learnt during this development period to help his family members and descendents in their progress in life.

Akashic records

Your life is said to be recorded in the spiritual realm within the Akashic records (Book of Life). According to mediums and seers, these are records of your present and all of your past lives or physical incarnations. Everything that has ever happened in the Universe is held in a vast library of the cosmic memory. It is thought that anyone who is capable of tuning in through psychic powers can access this memory bank.

THE GEOGRAPHY OF THE HUMAN BEING

Every human being has both a physical body that lives and is visible in the physical dimensions and other bodies that are only visible through Extra sensory perception (ESP). This chapter describes how we link to the invisible spirit planes and what a person looks like within the whole of the multi-dimensional Universe.

The auras

If you look at a person you see only the physical body. A psychic can see seven extra bodies, layers or auras surrounding it. These are only visible or detectable through extrasensory perception or clairvoyance.

Each aura is of a higher vibration or frequency. These bodies interlink and are as real as your physical body. If they are healthy, you will be healthy. If they are unhealthy, you will experience mental, spiritual, emotional or physical imbalance.

Each aura is believed to link to a different plane of the Universe.

Reading the auras

The second and third auras make up a field that is influenced by your belief systems, and values, and

	Name	Description
Seventh	Ketheric template/ causal body	Spiritual aura concerned with divine mind. When balanced you feel part of the great pattern of life.
Sixth	Celestial body	Spiritual aura concerned with divine love. When balanced, you feel joy and bliss.
Fifth	Etheric template	Spiritual aura concerned with divine will. When it is in balance you feel aligned with the order of things.
Fourth	Astral aura	The body is carried from life to life by us. It carries within it your intention to exist and to be – the cause of your existence.
Third	Mental aura	Concerned with thought. Disturbances and blocks in this field will show up in mental and emotional health.
Second	Emotional aura	Associated with your feelings and emotions. Eighteen inches from the body.
First	Etheric aura	Two to three inches from the physical body. Mirrors physical health of the body.

Colour	Plane	Related Chakra
Violet, becoming pure white or gold	Adi – level of God (oneness)	Crown
Indigo	Anupadaka – level of deities and highest levels of angels	Third Eye
Blue	Atmic – archangel, saint level	Throat
Green or pink	Buddhic – guardian angel level	Heart
Yellow	Rainbow – level of ancestors (heaven equivalent)	Solar plexus
Orange – changing colours that mirror emotional changes.	Astral – level of non-human guides	Sacral
Silver haze or red	Earth – level of dreams (meditation)	Base

Higher Planes

the emotions related to them. A psychic reading the auras at this level may pick up thoughts that are not conscious to the person being 'read' but that are unconsciously influencing his behaviour.

When reading the higher auras of the body, psychics can pick up messages about future events that will impact the person being read. This is because on an etheric level, events in the future already exist. These influences from the higher planes register within the auras of the body as they wait to be translated into real events.

A psychic can pick up a message about a big change or event affecting a group of people by tapping into the archetypal energies in the trans-personal field.

The feeling of being pushed or pulled by fate is also the influence of the higher cosmic forces. Any major change in an individual's life comes through the influence of changes flowing from this level.

The higher self

The three higher spiritual auric layers are the seat of the higher self. The higher self or superconscious is our personal link between the visible and invisible Universes. It is the part of us that links to the planes of archetypal or universal forces and energies. It communicates and inter-relates with higher cosmic consciousness.

The higher self transmits messages to the unconscious mind in the form of dreams, intuition and psychic insight. The unconscious then communicates these to your conscious mind through images, thoughts and feelings. Some of these images, for example those that occur in dreams and mediation, are symbolic and need interpretation.

It is possible to make this process more effective through psychic development exercises. By tuning in regularly to your unconscious, through meditation and visualisation exercises, you can become more comfortable with interpreting the language of the unconscious. As you open up your internal channels through improved communication between your conscious and unconscious, you also open up a clearer channel to your higher self.

The auras contain seven energy centres or vortexes known as the chakras. The word chakra comes from the Sanskrit meaning 'wheel'. According to ancient traditions, a chakra is where 216 energy channels (meridians or nadis) cross over to form life energy spirals. The Egyptians, Chinese, Hindus, Greeks, and Romans believed in the existence of the chakras.

The chakras link all levels of the aura and the physical body. Chakras one, two and three are concerned with a person's basic needs of survival and will. Chakras four to seven access and balance our emotional and psychological makeup. The highest chakra – the crown chakra – is the point of access to the spiritual Universe.

The chakras are connected to each other through etheric channels. The main channel runs in a vertical line from the base to the crown. As well as the main chakras, there are thousands of minor chakras throughout the body.

Chakra	Name (Sanskrit)	Situated	Colour
Seventh	Crown (sahasrara)	Top of the head	White, violet
Sixth	Third eye, brow, (ajna)	Between brows, behind forehead	Indigo
Fifth	Throat (visuddha)	Throat	Blue
Fourth	Heart (anahata)	Over the sternum	Green
Third	Solar plexus (manipura)	Above the naval	Yellow
Second	Sacral, sexual (svadhisthana)	Just below the nava	Orange
First	Root, base (muladhara)	Base of spine and the pubic bone	Red

Physical, emotional, mental or spiritual ailments can be correlated with energy blocks or dysfunctions within the chakras. Balancing the chakra through psychic healing allows the appropriate flow of energy to a chakra to re-establish health on each level.

Chakras have many correspondences, including planets, angels and deities, and sounds.

Governs	Central concern	Element
Personal source of divinity, gateway to God, spiritual will, enlightenment	Universal	Thought
Self-reflection, celestial body, intuition, vision, sixth sight, spirituality	Archetypal	Light
Self-expression, etheric body, creative power, self-expression, communication	Creative	Sound
Self-acceptance, love, understanding, balance, compassion	Social	Air
Self-definition, personal power, will, energy, emotional issues	Ego	Fire
Self-gratification, vital energy, change, separation, sexuality, creativity	Emotional	Water
Self-preservation, Kundalini, survival, grounding willpower, motivation	Physical	Earth

PSYCHICS AND MEDIUMS

Psychics

A psychic is someone who has powers to detect the invisible Universe, to foresee events in the future or to contact spirits.

There are many types of psychic powers. These are often grouped under titles such as sixth sense, extrasensory perception, inner sight or intuition. Those who have psychic powers have different names too. They may be called sensitives, intuitives, clairvoyants, mediums, or trance mediums.

Am I psychic?

Everybody has some psychic ability. If you have ever had a sense that something was going to happen in advance, you are tuning into your latent abilities. For example:

- Knowing who is about to phone you
- Knowing what a person is feeling or thinking
- Having an intuition or hunch that turns out to be correct

Psychic or mentally ill?

Is there a difference between someone who thinks they are psychic and someone who is mentally ill?

Throughout history, many people have been locked away on the grounds of insanity for saying they could talk to the spirits and other invisible beings.

There is a key difference between being psychic and being mentally ill: a person with psychic ability has a clear boundary between the 'real' physical world and the invisible world. A person who is schizophrenic, for example, cannot distinguish between what is in their head and what they observe around them in the material world.

Inner sight

The inner knowing that a psychic has is sometimes referred to as inner sight. Inner sight may refer to clairvoyance, but it also may refer simply to a psychic consciousness received through a variety of channels.

A psychic goes inside themselves, bypassing the conscious rational mind to reach the more abstract level or an inner recognition about a piece of information – a psychic message or impression.

Clairvoyance

Clairvoyance is used to mean a 'hunch' or gut feeling that something is going to happen that turns out to be correct. This is common to all of us. But most people don't consistently pay attention to their instincts. Logical, left-brain thinking is held in high regard by modern Western society. You can overturn this and learn to pay attention to your hunches and grow your clairvoyance.

Clairvoyant, **clairvoyant reader** and **clairvoyant psychic** are terms that also refer specifically to a person who has the ability to sense or intuit what is going on through sight. They can pick up visual images about a person, situation or event. Clairvoyance is regarded as the most widespread psychic ability and has been the most researched.

Clairvoyants may see auras and thought forms within the energy fields, as well as specific psychic phenomena such as guides, angels or other entities. Clairvoyants may also pick up visual symbols and images relating to the present, past or future as well as to physical, emotional or mental dysfunctions and illness.

Clairaudience, clear audio or clear hearing is the ability to sense though sounds, and voices.

Clairsentience is a predominantly kinesthetic sensing. Clear sensation, clear feeling, clairempathy and clear emotion are other terms used to describe aspects of this ability.

Clairtangency, clear touching is the ability to sense through touch. It relates to psychometry and clairsentience.

Clairgustance or clear tasting is the ability to sense through taste.

Clairscent or **clear smelling** is the ability to sense through smell.

Often psychic abilities will reveal themselves through a combination of images through the five senses.

Mediumship

Not everyone who is psychic is a medium. A medium is someone who can contact and receive messages from the spirit world. They may also have other powers including clairvoyance.

Famous Mediums

One of the most famous mediums of recent times is **Doris Stokes** (1920 –1987), a British medium who helped to make mediumship popular in the late twentieth century. She claimed to have started seeing spirits in childhood. Repeated attempts were made to prove her a fraud but none succeeded. In the 1970s she took part in a series of tests of her ability live on television in America, which raised her profile considerably.

More recently, television has helped to make other mediums famous. These include: **Derek Acorah**, a British medium who often appears on television and author of *The Psychic Adventures of Derek Acorah*

(2004) and *Ghost Hunting with Derek Acorah* (2005); **Gordon Smith**, 'the psychic barber', a Scottish medium who specialises in comforting the bereaved; **John Edward**, the host of the television show *Crossing Over*; and **Allison du Bois**, on whom the US hit show *Medium* is based, who has been used as a psychic for police work. She refers to herself as a 'profiler' and has spent four years being tested at the University of Arizona in their investigations of psychic phenomena.

How a medium communicates with spirits

The world of spirit exists in a dimension of a higher vibration. A medium forms a link or channel – a route of communication with those who have passed to the other side. He does this by raising his vibration or frequency to a point where a link can be formed. At the same time, the spirits lower their vibration. They communicate through the energies of pictures, feelings, sounds and thoughts. The medium interprets these through clairvoyance, clairsentience and clairaudience. This process is often called 'making a link'. The medium uses a doorkeeper spirit to facilitate the process and to protect him from negative energies. He may also use other helper spirit guides for specific purposes.

Readings/sittings

In a reading, a medium 'reads' or 'translates' the present, past or future situation of the sitter (the person who has come for a reading). A medium may pick up a picture of the spirit who is trying to communicate to the client.

The medium can make links to the spirit world more easily when the sitter is present, because the sitter's spirit guides and family may already be present at the start of the meeting, drawn to him by the opening up of the channel.

What to expect

A medium should be able to provide a recognisable physical or character description of a loved one who has died. The medium will enter into a light trance state to make the link. He then asks through internal thought, either directly or through his doorkeeper guide, for a spirit to come forward for the sitter. The medium is likely then to ask the spirit for proof of its identity or the spirit will offer proof in the form of a picture, thought or feeling. For example, a spirit may send a pain to the medium's body to show him where an illness is in the sitter, or how the spirit passed on to the afterlife.

The medium describes what he picks up and may ask the spirit whether it has any message. He can ask the spirit questions, but cannot make the spirit answer, or indeed stay present.

You can ask for specific messages about your career, relationships, family or any aspect of your life in the future, past or present.

Don't expect to see spirits (unless you are sensitive to them), tables being moved around the room, ectoplasm or anything spooky.

Tools

Many psychics use tools such as cards to facilitate spirit communication. These tools can also relate to a particular spirit guide that the medium likes to work with. For example, a South American guide may like to have an artefact present relating to its culture when it makes contact with the medium. Likewise, a piece of jewellery belonging to a family member who has died may draw his or her spirit to the reading.

Blocked communication

Even well-known mediums and those who are convinced that psychic powers are real admit that communication with the spirits is an inexact science. Sometimes information is received and understood easily. Sometimes it does not flow. This is because:

- The messages that come to the medium must be interpreted and are often obscure. The interpretation may distort the message.
- Sometimes the message relates to someone who is not present. This is almost like a

telephone call that has been misdirected by an exchange.

- If the message refers to a future event it cannot easily be validated.
- Some mediums cannot distinguish between a person who is still on the physical plane and someone who is in spirit. They have to ask the sitter to interpret the clues they have been given.
- Sometimes the reader is too closed-minded to hear the information, or they have come to the sitting with a set idea of who they would hear from or what they would hear.

However, often psychic mediums can come up with a detail like a name, or even address or personal memory about someone who has died that enables the listener to identify who the message is for.

Remote reading

A sitting can be face to face on the phone or even on the internet. They are connected by the spirit world and there is no time or space at this level of the Universe. The medium's spirit makes contact with the sitter's spirit and thoughts are sent to, and translated by the medium.

The purpose of mediumship

Mediums usually see themselves as having one of the following purposes:

- To prove the existence of a spirit world and afterlife.
- To help people through bereavement and grief.
- To help the soul's evolution on the physical plane.
- To advise others.
- To fulfill their own spiritual purpose.

Physical mediumship

Most modern mediums simply talk to their clients. In the early part of the twentieth century, however, the emphasis of mediumship was on providing physical evidence of the spirit world, for example through table-rapping and -tilting, as well as materialized spirit forms and levitation.

Physical Mediums

Helen Duncan (1898–1956) was a physical medium who was born in Scotland and became well known in the 1930s and '40s. In one of her famous cases, she made contact with the spirit of a sailor whom no one knew had died until the sinking of his ship was announced hours later. In 1944, one of her séances was raided by the police. She was accused firstly of being a fraud, then detained under the Witchcraft Act of 1735 and sentenced to nine months in prison. After her release, she returned to her work as a medium and in 1951 the Witchcraft Act was repealed and substituted with the Fraudulent Mediums Act. Up to her death, she continued to be accused of fraud but no claim was ever proven and there are many testimonials to her genuine ability.

Daniel Dunglas Home (1833–1886) was the most famous physical medium of the nineteenth century. Born in Scotland, he began attracting psychic activity after moving to America. He conducted open séances, with levitations, furniture moving and objects materialising on stage. Despite being accused of being a fraud, even the famed magician Harry Houdini could not replicate many of his feats.

Rescue mediumship

Rescue mediums specialise in helping spirits who are stuck in transition in finding their way. The theory is that some souls become confused when they pass over to the afterlife. This may be because of a violent death, or because the person is unable to accept they have died. A rescue medium guides the soul to the light – the higher frequencies.

Trance mediumship

Trance mediums channel a spirit guide through their voice. The spirit guide comes directly into the aura of the medium. In some cases the medium is seen to be in a sleep-like state. In others, the medium is apparently conscious and alert to what is happening.

Overshadowing: the spirit guide uses the voice of the medium to communicate but the content/words come directly from the spirit guide.

Inspired speaking: the medium chooses the exact words but channels information or inspiration from the spirit guide who has entered into his aura.

Trance: the medium will contact his guide. The medium then appears to fall asleep. After a few moments the spirit guide begins to speak through the medium in the voice the spirit has chosen, for example in a foreign accent. When the medium 'awakes' he will often be unaware of what has been said.

How do I become a medium?

Some mediums are born with the ability. Others acquire the skill in childhood or as an adult, sometimes recognising the skill after contact with another medium. Often a medium will have had hardship in his life as part of his own spiritual development.

You can train your ability to be a medium if you have a natural talent. But although we all have some psychic powers, not all of us have the ability to be a medium.

Are you a medium?

Some signs of latent and developing mediumship:

- Inherited ability from a parent or grandparent who was a medium.
- Other mediums say that you have the ability to be a medium.
- You frequently hear voices internally or externally calling out to you or talking to you.
- You see milky white mists in your home.
- You feel as if you are being touched by cold hands.
- You attract paranormal activity around you, for example electrical appliances turning themselves on and off.
- You frequently see spirits around you at night.

Spiritualism

This book concentrates on the development of general psychic powers. To develop as a medium, one of the safest places to go is a Spiritualist church.

The main purpose of Spiritualism is to prove that life exists after death. During Spiritualist Sunday services, a medium is invited to channel messages for the congregation from spirits who have 'passed over.' Churches also often provide healing for people and animals on other days, as well as workshops.

Medium circles

Churches may provide development circles (a group) of mediums. In a group, you may tune into a spirit guide more easily than elsewhere, as the vibration of the group will be high and the spirits will be easier to contact. In a circle you can learn how to separate instinct from imagination.

Services in Spiritualist churches are simple and are based on seven core beliefs and principles. Summarised, these are:

- The fatherhood of God.
- The brotherhood of Man.
- The communion of spirits and the ministry of angels.
- The human soul has a continuous existence.
- Each person has personal responsibility.
- We will receive compensation and retribution for all the deeds done upon the earth.
- Eternal progress is open to every human soul.

There is no set time scale for how long mediumship training takes. It may take weeks, months or a year or more.

To find a spiritualist church or medium, contact the Spiritualist Association of Great Britain – SAGB. **http://www.sagb.org.uk**

FINDING A PSYCHIC

You can find a medium through recommendation or through a local spiritualist church. Many psychics advertise, however you should be careful about anyone who charges exorbitant fees, and always go by your instinct. There are frauds out there. You would not go to an unlicensed doctor or professional. Use the same discrimination to pick a suitable medium/psychic. Listen to your gut instinct. A good psychic will 'feel' right.

The role of a psychic

A psychic is there to advise you and to help you to act in accordance with your highest interest. Even if he predicts an event in the future you can choose out of free will to change direction or to block it. Sometimes the advice given may sound unspecific. The ability of each psychic to pick up and interpret messages varies.

Paying for psychic information

A frequent question is why psychics charge fees when they are providing a spiritual service for their clients. Some psychics see this as a necessary exchange of energy with the client. Others make their living from giving readings, and so charge as they would in any another job.

Warning: You will still find fraudulent psychics. Here are some warning signals:

• The psychic is more interested in your money than the reasons you are seeing him.
• He tells you that your future will definitely happen in a particular way if you take certain actions. A psychic can foretell probabilities but no future is set in stone: people will always have free will.
• He asks too many personal questions – a genuine psychic does not need to know this information. He relies on the information he receives from his extrasensory powers.
• He guarantees a specific result, for example that he can contact a dead relative. A genuine psychic cannot guarantee results.

Cold reading

Critics of psychics and mediums attribute the positive results they get to cold reading. This is a technique that is used by mentalists (people who pretend to be able to read minds and predict events), con men and sales people.

Here's how it works:

Shotgunning: A fraudulent psychic may give a huge quantity of information, some of which is likely to be correct. According to the sitter's reaction, they then refine the information.

Eliciting cooperation: The psychic starts by suggesting a number of images that are vague and asks the sitter to make sense of them. He follows the sitter's lead in the information they provide.

Hot reading: The fraudulent psychic uses covertly gathered information together with cold reading techniques.

The *Forer effect* is the term given to an individual who will believe a description of their character that seems to be tailored for them, but is in fact general enough to fit a huge range of people. The effect works if the subject believes in the authority of the psychic and if the analysis is mainly positive.

DEVELOPING YOUR PSYCHIC POWERS

Psychic abilities can be developed. There are many exercises you can do to develop your abilities, and the exercises in this chapter can be used by anyone. The more you practise the easier it becomes. At first, the psychic information you notice may appear trivial. It doesn't matter. If you have a sense, see a picture or hear a message, follow up. This will help to open up your psychic channels.

Accept you will be wrong, sometimes or often at first. Practise every day if you can, just as you would if you were learning a new language or to play an instrument. Mediums are called instruments of the spirit for a reason.

Recognising psychic powers

What are your expectations of psychic abilities? How will you know whether you are developing your powers? Many beginners find that their abilities are completely unpredictable at first. Don't worry about controlling your abilities, just notice that *some* change is happening. Start by recognising that psychic information is coming your way.

Signs of developing ability:

- Strong or sudden intuitions or feelings about a person, place or object.
- A deep certainty that takes over your whole being.
- Synchronicities and coincidences occurring in your life.
- Perceiving patterns of events and experiences.

Principles of psychic powers

Psychic powers operate within a set of principles. These underlie and ensure the success of all the techniques you will learn in this and subsequent chapters.

We live in a thought Universe

All the ancient esoteric systems agree that the Universe is controlled by the power of conscious and unconscious thought. In other words, thoughts can translate into reality. When you use your psychic powers, you will deliberately use thought and intention to cause something to manifest (come into physical existence) in the material world. You can and do create your future. For example, a prayer or a spell, formulated in the right way, is heard within the invisible Universe and is realised within the material world (though often after a time gap).

This means that you have the power to make anything possible. The only limits are your own beliefs about what you can ask the Universe for.

If you doubt that the Universe will give you what you ask for, the doubt will be realised as the doubt itself is a powerful thought. Likewise, any unconscious beliefs about your psychic powers can act as blocks to the development of those powers.

Thought is a potent energy that can be used for ill as well as good. Once a thought exists, it exists forever. It cannot be un-thought because although it may no longer be on this plane it still exists as energy on other levels of the Universe. As you develop as a psychic, the message is to be aware and to be careful about what you are thinking, because every thought that you have is heard in the invisible Universe. Since the Universe does not distinguish between a positive and a negative thought, a negative thought will draw a negative manifestation towards you.

Karma

In some religions there exists the idea of karma – a Sanskrit word that means 'cause and effect'. This is usually interpreted as meaning that in this life you reap the rewards or punishment for actions in past lives. A more useful principle is the idea that you are what you are in the moment, and any karma that exists, exists in relation to your actions now. In other words, take responsibility for how you think and act now. The only current limits are the ones you impose on yourself.

Everything is interconnected

When you use psychic power, you tap into the level of the Universe where individuality doesn't exist. At this level, each of us is part of a universal and cosmic consciousness where we are connected as though held together by invisible threads.

This inter-connectedness means that everything we do or think affects everything and everyone else. A black magician uses this knowledge to send negative thoughts that will harm another person. Telepathy uses it to pick up messages about someone at a distance. Telekinesis uses it to produce psychic phenomena at a distance.

The Universe is made up of energy

Everything is made up of energy: what appears to be solid is made up of vibrating particles, atoms and molecules. This includes human beings. According to psychic theory, all the beings that live in the Universe are made up of vibrating energies. The higher and faster the frequency, the higher the plane of the Universe.

Psychic development will teach you how to raise and lower your vibration at will. This allows communication with spirits of higher frequencies and also means that you can direct and change energies through extrasensory powers. Spoon-bending and telekinesis are examples of this.

There is only now

Time and space are features of the material world, not the invisible world. At higher levels of the Universe there is no time or space. The present, past and future are all occurring right now. This means that when you contact the higher realms you can tap into past lives, or the future.

All power exists inside you

Once you understand these basic principles, you will realise that the power to draw on all of the resources of the invisible and visible Universes exists inside you.

By learning to project your will and change your vibration through altering your state of consciousness, you will begin to develop your psychic powers. That power is already within you. You simply may not have realised it yet.

The exercises that follow will help you to develop your belief in yourself as a psychic and through this develop your powers in a safe way.

Although you may learn to work with tools, spirits or guides throughout these exercises, you are the real power. They are all simply useful extras that help to free you up from any belief constraints that you normally have in your everyday existence. If they help you to develop your abilities use them. If they don't, leave them.

ALPHA STATE

All psychic exercises require you to alter your state of consciousness to reach the alpha state.

Beta: In everyday life, our brains generally function at a level of activity known as the beta level. At this level, the brain has a rhythm of electrical activity of between 13 and 30 cycles per second. The beta level allows us to be conscious and take in the information we need during the day.

Alpha: The alpha state is a light trance state where the electrical activity of the brain is less: between 7 and 13 cycles per second. We naturally go into the alpha state when we relax or day-dream. It can also be induced through meditation and hypnosis.

This is the best level for psychically tuning in to the auras or the spirit.

Theta: The level below the alpha level is the theta level. Here brain activity reduces to 4 to 7 cycles per second. The theta state is the level of a deep trance state – the state hypnosis uses to achieve surgical anaesthesia. As you become skilled at reaching alpha level, you may dip down into theta on occasions.

While many experienced psychics can move from beta to alpha levels at will, those of us who are not as practised need to develop this habit through meditation and exercise. Once you can do this you can start to develop other specific psychic techniques.

Signs of alpha state

You will recognise when you are at the alpha level as your awareness changes. Time seems to pass at a different rate, you cease to notice noise and visual distractions around you, and your breathing slows. You may have a heightened awareness of colour, feelings of love within yourself, or an expansiveness and sense of connectedness with all things.

Meditation

Meditation is the best way to begin to develop your ability to focus for a sustained length of time at the alpha level of the mind.

The word meditation derives from the Latin root 'med-', from measure. There are many styles of meditation. Some use a 'mandala' or other object to develop focus, or a word repeated in the mind. Self-hypnosis is also a form of meditation in which the mind is stilled to reach an altered state of consciousness.

Power is in the now

All the psychic techniques you will learn are based on one idea: be present in the now.

Many people are not in the moment. Their attention and awareness fluctuates and flicks back and forth from the current moment to memories of the past or visions of the future. To be truly present in the moment will give you tremendous power. Altering your state of consciousness through the different techniques will allow you to be totally present in your experience of every second and minute, becoming aware of how you are feeling, the colours you can see, the sounds you can hear, the smells and tastes.

Music

Different music has different vibrations as has been shown clearly through research such as the 'Mozart effect' (the therapeutic effect of Mozart's music on health and well-being). Chanting and certain pieces of music, especially some classical music, can raise your vibration and help you to mediate. Experiment and see what music works for you. But be careful if the music has lyrics – make sure they are positive.

THE FOUNDATION EXERCISES

The alpha state exercise

Practise this for around 15 to 30 minutes when you first start, especially if you have never meditated before. You can do this exercise at any time of day.

Part One

1 First choose somewhere comfortable to sit. It is better to sit with your arms and legs relaxed rather than to lie down, so that you only go into the alpha state rather than fall asleep.

2 Make sure your clothing is loose and comfortable and your arms are resting on your lap or on the arms of the chair. Make sure your legs feel well supported in the ground. Keep your legs uncrossed.

3 Close your eyes.

4 Take a few deep, long breaths in and out so that you begin to slow down your breathing. Let your breath go deeper. Feel the relaxation begin to flow with your breath through your body.

5 First notice how heavy your head feels, then your neck. Let go of all the tension in your neck, and notice how light your head and neck now feel.

6 Become aware of your arms and shoulders, feel them becoming heavy and relaxed. Release the tension and feel them become light.

7 Become aware of your torso and your stomach. Feel the tension release.

8 Become aware of your legs and feet. Notice the tension in them. Feel them become heavy, and then as you release the tension into the air around you, they become light.

9 Now your whole body is light and relaxed.

Part Two
1 Next, deepen your state. Imagine that you are in a place of relaxation, somewhere that is utterly peaceful for you. This might be the countryside, or lying on a beach or another scene in your mind's eye. Spend some time here, enjoying what you see, hear and feel.

2 You should now have reached the alpha state. Spend as long as you want to here.

Part Three
1 When you want to come out of the state, count from one to five in your mind.

2 At the count of two, begin to increase your breathing.

3 At the count of three, allow the breath to awaken your body.

4 At the count of four, begin to become fully aware of your body again.

5 At the count of five, open your eyes. Notice how you feel, and get up slowly!

As you become more familiar with the alpha state, you will find that you can reach it very quickly just by closing your eyes, taking a few breaths and relaxing your mind and body.

Basic white light exercise

This exercise will help you to open up your energetic bodies to receive higher vibrational energy and to start to tune your awareness of the other planes. It is also an energetic cleansing and preparation exercise. White light is the pure love energy of the Universe.

Practise this daily. Although this is a very basic exercise, you can also integrate this into some of the later, more advanced exercises.

1 See a beam of light above your head coming down

Basic white light exercise

from the Universe, as if you are standing below a spotlight on stage.

2 Now imagine that you can open up the top of your head (your crown chakra).

3 Feel the light shine down through the crown chakra and flow down through your whole body, through your head, your torso, your stomach, your arms and hands, legs and feet into the ground.

4 As the light flows through your body, you can see

or feel it filling up your whole body so that your whole body is filled to the brim with white light.

5 The white light flows into your auras – cleaning all levels of your auras.

6 Any darkness or dullness is cleaned away into the earth below you.

7 Come out of the alpha state when you have finished the process. You should feel fresh and invigorated and full of loving, peaceful energy.

Basic visualisation exercise

Visualising is a great aid to enhancing your psychic powers. Learning to 'see' inside your head is the foundation of more advanced techniques.

1 Sit quietly, take a few deep breaths and relax your body. Take yourself to your alpha state.

2 In your mind's eye imagine that you can see a screen in front of you above your eye level.

3 Imagine that you can take a pen or pencil and write the number 1 on the screen.

4 Now, write your name.

5 Next, see yourself on the screen.

6 Add another positive image to the picture of your own choosing.

7 Clear the screen and open your eyes.

8 Come back to full awareness.

You can practise this exercise whenever you like. Make positive pictures in your mind of happy scenes that you would like to have in your future. The more detail you can visualise the more skilled you will become. Add colour, sights, sounds and feelings to your pictures.

Tell yourself, 'I am skilled at visualising'.

Becoming familiar with the chakras exercise

Learn how to open and close your chakras. Whenever you want to open up to higher energies open up your chakras. To lower your vibration again after a psychic exercise, close your chakras.

Sit down in a chair, close your eyes and relax. Take a deep breath.

1 In your mind, focus on your base chakra. See the energy of the chakra circling around. Visualise the chakra with petals like a lotus flower full to the brim with white light. Imagine the petals opening up and

then closing into a tight bud. Feel the difference in your energy field as the chakra is opened and closed.

2 Next, focus on your sacral chakra immediately below your navel. Open and close the petals.

3 Next, open and close the petals of the solar plexus chakra, above your navel.

4 Move to the heart chakra and do the same.

5 Next, move to the throat chakra. Open and close it.

6 Now move to the brow or third eye chakra. Open and close it.

7 Finally, take your attention to the crown chakra on top of your head.

8 Notice any differences among the chakras and how each one feels when it is closed or open.

The third eye is a point between your two eyebrows. Many religions say that activating the third eye is the source of perfect knowledge and spiritual enlightenment. This may be because this is the location of the pineal gland, which scientists know to be affected by light. In the Eastern Tantrika system, the third eye is the Ajna chakra that is white coloured and has two petals. In other systems, this chakra is indigo coloured. According to the *Eastern Tantrika* system, when you open this chakra, you gain the power to command what you will to happen in the world.

Opening your third eye will:

- Increase your intuition and awareness.
- Build your will to influence outcomes.
- Develop ESP.

How to open your third eye exercise

1 Close your eyes. Take a few deep breaths and relax down into an altered (alpha) state.

2 With your eyelids closed and keeping your face relaxed, move your eyes as if you are looking up at the point between your two eyebrows. Touch this point with the finger-tips of your right hand.

3 By rolling your eyes up, you may be aware of white light at this point. If this is slow in coming, then relax your eyes. Slowly and very

Third eye exercise

gently massage your third eye in a clockwise direction.

4 As your third eye opens up, you will see white or indigo light. Gradually, other colours may emerge.

5 As the psychic channel becomes stronger and the curtains of the third eye are drawn, it is as though you are looking at a screen of images and visions.

6 Watch the screen for not more than ten minutes.

Closing down exercise

Every time you do any psychic exercise, close down your third eye and protect yourself. Here is a simple method:

1 See the petals of your third eye closing up. Cover it in purple light.

2 Finally wrap your whole body in a cloak of white light.

3 Gradually feel yourself in your body again. Move your legs and arms. Feel yourself fully grounded and rooted in the material world.

4 You can imagine roots coming out of your feet and growing deep into the earth.

5 Open your eyes and be fully awake.

COLOURS

Visualising colour

Becoming aware of different colours will help you to connect with your different chakras and increase the accuracy of any visualisation you do in a meditative state by connecting you to the senses.

Colour exercise

1 Sit quietly. Close your eyes, take a few deep breaths and relax into your alpha state.

2 Visualise a wall in front of you. Notice what colour it is.

3 Now take a paint brush in your mind and paint it red.

4 Next paint it orange.

5 Then yellow.

6 Then green.

7 Then blue.

8 Then indigo.

9 Finally violet.

10 Now see all the colours of the rainbow in stripes on the wall.

11 Open your eyes.

The psychic qualities of colour

You may find that at particular times one colour will feel more appropriate for you than another. You may be drawn to wear that colour, or buy objects for the home of that colour.

This may be because you need some of this colour to tune into the qualities of a particular plane of existence, to balance a chakra or your whole aura, or to protect yourself from psychic energies.

Experiment with the feeling of different colours. Instead of a white light, try surrounding yourself with red or pink, purple, yellow, gold or green. How does each colour feel? Which is appropriate for you at the moment? A different colour will have a real effect on your mood.

Religious and mystical leaders have long known the power of colour. Rituals such as weddings and funerals demand one colour rather than another, because every colour has its own vibration and power. In esoteric tools such as the Tarot, colour is used alongside symbols to unconsciously tune in the reader to higher psychic vibrations.

These are some of the main correspondences of different colours:

White: purity, life. It contains all the other colours and reflects back what is sent towards it.
Red: energy, courage, self-confidence.
Orange: confidence, independence, sociability. Orange stimulates the appetite.
Yellow: wisdom, clarity. Yellow relieves depression and helps memory.
Green: love, peace, relaxation, serenity. Relieves depression and anxiety.
Blue: femininity, passivity, harmony. Blue enhances communication.
Indigo: intuition, imagination. Indigo connects to the unconscious.
Violet: wisdom, creativity, kindness.
Gold: positivity, forceful sun energy. Gold represents action, and will balance disturbed energy.

Clothing

Wear light-coloured clothes to attract light-coloured energies as your psychic powers become more attuned. It will keep you feeling in a better state of wellbeing on all levels. Black and other dark clothes suppress your mood and may leave you feeling depleted.

DREAMS

Over the first few weeks, as you begin to practise developing your abilities, it is useful to record your dreams so that you notice any recurring or unusual symbols. Improving your dream recall will make it easier for you to relate to and analyse any intuition that comes from your meditation practice.

Keep a dream journal

Some people remember their dreams easily. Others are barely aware of dreaming. To improve your dream recall, carry out dream exercises regularly.

1 Each night before you go to sleep, take a few minutes with your eyes closed to remember what has happened through the day. Mentally play through a film of the events that have happened to you. Watch the film impartially as if you are a detached observer of a film.

2 See yourself falling asleep and sleeping deeply and peacefully before waking up and recording your dreams.

3 For the first week, keep a dream journal. Prompt your unconscious to be ready to remember your dreams by keeping a pen and notebook by your bed.

4 When you wake up, write down as much as you can remember of the details of what happened. Make sure you do this as soon as you awake. Your recall will be much sharper. If you are lacking in time, you can just write the main turning points in the narrative or any highlights of the story and fill in the details later.

5 At the end of the week, look back at your dream notes. Note down any main themes and highlights. Pay attention to any symbols or characters.

6 Think about the relationship between what you

dreamt and your current mental, emotional, physical and spiritual state. Can you identify any messages in the dreams about your current state?

After you have recorded your dreams over a longer period and begun to tune in to your psychic abilities in other ways, you will find it easier to notice the difference between run-of-the-mill dreams and those that contain any significant psychic pointers or clues as to further personal development you need.

Lucid dreams

Lucid dreaming is being aware of dreaming in the middle of a dream. You can control how the dream progresses and what you dream about. This could be for problem solving, or self-growth, or to aid communication in a relationship.

You can use lucid dreaming to talk to a particular person in dream state, or to explore a situation.

1 To practise lucid dreaming. Ask before you go to sleep that you become aware of the moment when you begin to dream. Ask for a particular symbol to alert you to wake up within the dream.

2 When you wake and become aware that you are in a dream, assert that you are directing the dream towards the area you wish to explore and note any answers.

PSYCHIC PROTECTION

Have you ever felt drained around a particular person or particular people? Do you sleep badly or feel uneasy in particular places? Have you ever felt a sudden drop in your energy or a stab to your heart or back when you read or hear something someone has said about you?

As you develop your sensitivity to the higher vibrations, one of the side effects you will experience is sensitivity to all energies; not only to those you wanted to attract.

At the early stages of psychic development, it is like being able to tune into a new TV channel without being able to turn down the volume or control the brightness. As a result, you receive all sorts of input you would rather not have. Some of these energies are positive, but some may not be.

It is essential to ground and protect yourself from subtle energies when developing psychically. Even if the energy is not essentially bad, you can take on too much energy, and negative energy may result in depression or illnesses (such as chronic fatigue syndrome or pains in the stomach), or the feeling of simply not being able to cope.

Psychic attack

Psychic attack is an intentional, or unintentional, negative psychic energy directed towards you.

Every time someone thinks about you with negativity they are attacking you psychically to a degree. A thought form is created out of the emotion. When the person thinks about your name, they link into your personal energy field and direct the thought towards you.

Unintentional attack

Unintentional thought forms may build up in a particular place if many people have felt fear or anger or another negative emotion such as depression there. That's how some buildings, such as a prison or doctor's surgery, can make you feel drained if you are sensitive to vibrations. The thought forms are not necessarily directed at a person, but stay in the building.

Particular professions such as social work, police work, medicine and therapy can have high sickness rates because employees deal with so many people who are feeling negative. Psychic and spiritual workers can easily become drained by their clients if they do not protect their energy and power.

Deliberate attack

Deliberate attacks come in two forms:

Psychic draining by a controlling or abusive person. A physical or emotional abuser deliberately tries to control other individuals. To a psychic this will be felt as an attack on the psychic level.

Black magic: You may be attacked by a psychic who is misusing their powers. This kind of attack is particularly dangerous when deliberately projected by a formal ritual or spell. Many ancient magicians thought it was dangerous for anyone to know their true name, because another magician could detect their personal vibration by creating a spell linked to their name. An intentional psychic attack can be felt in a particular part of the body or may result in mental illness. This type of attack also includes voodoo dolls.

Be careful of your thoughts

Be careful about what you are thinking. You are as capable of attacking someone as you are of being attacked.

If you are upset with someone, make sure you catch the thought and dissolve it by immediately surrounding the person with white light. At the same time, thank them for the situation that has given rise to your thoughts. Thank yourself for your reaction to the situation and forgive both yourself and the person you are upset with. This will dissolve the thought form.

You can also attack yourself with your own thoughts.

1 Cleanse yourself of any dark holes you blow into your own aura with your thoughts by regular meditation and use of the white light exercise.

2 Strengthen your positive power in the world. Imagine that as you go through life you radiate positive light to the world as if you are the sun, glowing with golden light. Practise walking into a party or a social situation radiating light and notice how drawn people are to you.

Psychic protection

Make it a habit to protect yourself psychically on a daily level. The most important thing you can do is to think positive loving thoughts.

A negative energy is cancelled out by a positive energy of the same or greater power. Positive thoughts, intentions and words all create positive energy.

You can't fight a negative attack with another negative attack for two reasons. First, it increases the negativity's power because like attracts like. The negativity will feed on the negativity you give it. Second, the law of the Universe is that if you think negatively about someone it will come back threefold on you. So if you think negatively about someone, it will rebound on you. The only thing you can do is to use loving energy to dissolve the negative thought form.

Practise

Remember to practise the different methods consistently. Doing something only once won't necessarily be effective in countering the attack.

Before you begin a psychic exercise, spend a few moments making sure that your aura is balanced and that you are surrounded by protective energies. When you open up your chakras to the higher frequencies, surround yourself with white light at the same time.

Detecting attack

If you are ill, you are not necessarily under attack, but you may be. Other indicators are suddenly encountering a run of bad luck, depression, or simply feeling drained. You may also have an intuition about someone's feelings towards you; this could alert you to something being wrong. If you are in doubt, do the exercises anyway and maintain a loving attitude. In the case of suspicions about an attack through magic, call on more developed psychics for help. But don't be paranoid about other people's motives. Many of your experiences may just be tests from the Universe and Spirit to strengthen your abilities and aid your personal development.

Exercises to protect yourself

There is an enormous range of rituals and practices you can use to protect yourself psychically. All these methods will strengthen your aura so that you can tune out disturbing energies while tuning into the higher vibrations you want to pick up.

White light

The simplest way of protection is for you to regularly surround yourself with white light. Just as light dissolves darkness, loving energy cancels out any attack that is thrown at you. Negative thought forms cannot penetrate white light – the purest form of positively charged energy in the Universe.

When you detect that you are being attacked, send the person attacking you continual white light.

White light exercise

1 When you wake up in the morning, imagine that you are enclosed in a bubble of white light. If it helps you to visualise, you can imagine that the bubble sits on top of a gold base under your feet.

2 See the white light extending to about 2 feet around your body, around your head and underneath your feet.

3 Make sure that this light is above your head, as well as under your feet.

4 Imagine the light is encircling you and then stationary, then swirling around you again.

5 Open your eyes and feel the white light protecting you.

To calm yourself down when you are negative, imagine that you are breathing in white light and emptying out of your body any dirty or dark energies.

Each time you walk out of the house, put the bubble around you once more. You can also extend this protection to your home, or a car or train or aircraft you are travelling in.

If you think a family member or loved one needs protection, see them surrounded by white light as well.

This is an extended version of the white light bubble.

Extended white light exercise

1 Sit or stand. Visualise the colours of the chakras running from the base chakra up to the crown. Imagine a ray of light emanating from each vortex.

2 See the red of the root, the orange of the sacral, the yellow of the solar plexus, the green of the heart, the blue of the throat, the indigo of the brow and the violet of the crown.

3 The rays merge together a few feet in front of you at eye level to become once again the white light out of which they originated.

4 Visualise yourself feeding this light point with positive psychic energy.

5 Grow it into a ball of light all around you and protecting you.

6 Now visualise a golden ray painting the whole sphere like a golden shield. This is your psychic shield that will open you up to all that is positive but repel the negative.

7 You can polish the gold to keep it shiny. Or you can paint a cross on the back as a symbol of God energy. Other religious symbols also work.

The power of intention

Since intention creates power, state your intention clearly each time you use white light. Simply say, 'I surround myself with the white light of God's love and protection' to seal your aura. Or 'I affirm that no force or frequency that is not of the light can enter my energy field'. This safeguards you against any energies of lower vibrations, such as thought forms from people dead or alive.

You can also call upon your spirit guide or the angels or God to protect you and to surround you with love and light at any time you feel vulnerable. Using the word God ensures that the vibration you receive is of the highest level.

Strengthening the aura before sleep

1 Ask for healing on a physical, mental, spiritual and emotional level, on all planes and on all levels. Ask for protection against all that is not of the light.

2 Imagine and ask that you are surrounded by white light.

3 Ask that all those who need light in their life receive it. Direct the light also to anyone that you have felt negative about in the past or who may be opposed to your spiritual and psychic development.

Violet flame

If you are in an office where you keep coming into contact with people who are directly or indirectly negative towards you, you can also call upon the violet flame of transmutation to burn the energy and turn it into white light.

The violet flame is also known as the Seventh Ray or the Violet Flame of St Germain. St Germain is an Ascended Master – a spirit at a higher level of development – who gave the knowledge of the ray to Guy Ballard (1878–1939) in the 1930s as a preparation for man's entry into the Age of Aquarius.

It is believed that spiritual light is refracted as seven rays, each of which has its own vibration, colour and qualities.

PROTECTION RITUALS

Try out different ways of protecting yourself psychically and see which you feel most comfortable with. They are all effective.

A ritual is a symbolic expression of your intention. With any ritual, ultimately it is your intention that is important, not the ritual itself. But performing the ritual creates shifts in your consciousness and may help you to make sudden leaps in your development.

Rituals do not have to be complicated. Even a simple daily affirmation can be a ritual. Just affirm

White candle ritual

your intention to link to the spiritual realms. Intend that the results will be positive for you and for the world at large.

Here are some possible rituals:

White candle

The simplest ritual is to light a white candle. Sit in front of it and imagine that you can breathe in the white light of the candle so it fills up and seals your aura.

Scent

Use scents to clean and protect the aura. Light an incense stick, smudge stick or incense on charcoal.

Reach into the scent with your hands. Waft it into your aura; pull the scent all around you body. Imagine it swirling around your head, over your body and under your feet. Inhale the aroma.

You can use this to clean a space in which you are working as well. Smudge or waft the scent around. State your intention to clear away any negative energies or blocks to your links with the Spirit so that you can clearly hear any messages you need.

Casting a circle

Before meditating, clear and protect your space. Cast a circle using salt, crystals or the Major Arcana Tarot cards around you. Or simply walk around in a circle affirming your intention to create this space.

State: 'I ask that this circle be filled with white light and love. I call upon the energies of the light to guide and protect me. I ask any negative energies to now leave this circle. Thank you God.'

Mirrors

Mirrors can be used to mirror an attack away from you. A simple way of doing this is to first put your white bubble in place around you. Next, imagine it is surrounded by mirrors facing outwards. Imagine that any energy hitting the mirrors bounces off the surface and reflects into the heavens where it dissolves.

A real mirror can also be used. If you know an attack is coming from a particular direction, put a mirror in the window so it faces outwards in that direction. Ask: 'Mirror protect this household and all who live here from harm.'

Crystals

Crystals can also be used for protection. Any crystal you buy from a New Age shop will do, but some of the best to use for protection purposes are clear quartz crystal, obsidian and hematite. Usually the different names and qualities of crystals are on display if you don't recognise which crystal is which.

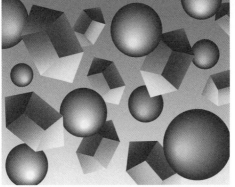

Crystals can be used for protection

The golden cross

If you feel that you are being attacked by a negative spirit energy or simply want to find out whether a spirit is 'of the light', as soon as you feel or see the spirit in contact with you, visualise a golden cross and place it around the neck of the spirit. A spirit that is not of God energy will not be able to stay with the cross and will leave you.

BLOCKS TO YOUR PSYCHIC LEARNING

You may be feeling pleased with what you are discovering about the spirit world when suddenly you meet a block – you don't remember your dreams, you can't sense any more, there are no synchronicities that you can observe in your life. Don't worry. This is very common before moving to the next stage of development where you may discover a new gift, or perhaps be contacted by a new guide.

Taking care of yourself

You need to take care of your physical self when you develop your psychic self. Make sure you eat healthily and exercise regularly. You don't have to adopt a particular diet, but you may become more sensitive to the low energies of junk food or food that is high in additives, and naturally gravitate towards food with higher nutrition and higher vibrations.

Blessing your food by holding one or both hands over it while asking for energy to be given to the food will raise its vibration and the positive effects on your wellbeing.

Drugs

Drugs, alcoholic drink and any mood-altering substance will affect your ability to receive clear psychic messages. Moreover, you will put yourself in danger of attracting spirits of low energy who can gain influence over you.

Some shamanistic traditions use drugs in ritual but in a very controlled and protected way. You do not have this protection.

Warning

All psychics must learn how to respect others and to take responsibility for the service they provide, as they often deal with vulnerable clients. It is vital that as your ability grows you do not become arrogant or egotistical, as this may lead you to follow a wrong path with your powers that will ultimately have karmic consequences for you.

ADVANCED PSYCHIC TECHNIQUES

Reading auras

To a clairvoyant, an aura looks like a colourful energy field extending outwards from the physical body by several feet. The different colours you see in someone's aura are a reflection of a person's mental, emotional, physical and spiritual health. Some may be bright, like the colours of the rainbow. Others may be dull. Dark spots in the aura may indicate an illness.

Science

Auras can be photographed. In the 1930s, a Russian electrician, Seymon Kirlian, took photographs of his hand. The pictures showed a glowing energy field around the hand. Modern researchers use electrical equipment to show these energy fields. This is known as Kirlian photography.

Seeing your own aura exercise

1 Sit in a dark room so that you are facing the wall. The room doesn't need to be pitch black, but make sure you turn out the main lights.

2 Hold both of your hands parallel to each other up in

front of your face at about half an arm's length distance. They should be as far apart as if they could hold a ball between them.

3 Look past your hands to the wall. As you do this, move your hands close together and apart again several times.

4 You will begin to see or feel the energy field between your hands. This will be seen as a colour or light or felt as a sensation.

Seeing someone else's aura exercise

1 Ask a friend to stand in front of a white wall. Relax and open your third eye with your mind. Imagine the petals of your third eye opening up.

2 Half close your eyes. Don't look directly, but scan the person's body starting at the head. Notice how far from the body their energy field stretches.

3 Notice any colours that you see in the energy field. The colours may not be consistent down the whole body and may change with movement.

4 Look for the dullness or brightness in the aura. Notice what your instinct tells you about any meaning to the colours.

TELEPATHY

Telepathy is the method by which you can communicate with another person through thought. You can receive or send information. Mind reading is a form of telepathy by which you use psychic power to detect what is in someone else's mind.

Telepathy can be spontaneous. For example, you may suddenly pick up a call in your mind from someone who is in danger. You can also intentionally communicate with another person.

Telepathy exercise

1 Pick a person (the receiver) with whom you agree to communicate. They do not have to be physically present but when you first begin it is easier if they are.

2 You (the sender) focus on a shape, picture or playing card.

3 Go to your alpha state. Imagine you are linking to the receiver through your third eye. Clear your mind except for the picture you are looking at. Imagine sending the picture to the receiver.

4 The receiver writes or draws what they receive.

5 Now change your roles around.

You may find you are better at receiving or sending messages. Or there may be a difference when the sender and receiver are physically together.

Psychic messages

A clairvoyant picks up messages in visual symbols, some of which are very common. You may find these symbols appearing when you meditate on a person or place, or in your dreams, or when you have a sitter in front of you.

These symbols can have both universal and personal meanings – and the personal meanings may relate to either the psychic or the sitter.

Common symbols

Colours: colours may be seen in the aura or as shapes within your inner field of vision.
Personal symbols: you may pick up symbols that are personal to you or a sitter. If you are reading for another person, it is important that you relay what the symbol is, without personal judgement if you are in any way unsure how to interpret it. It may be a significant object or person, place or situation. For example, a particular object may be linked to a memory.
Archetypal symbols: these include many of the images found in the Tarot, especially the esoteric versions of the Tarot such as the cards drawn in the

Tarot Death card

Golden Dawn traditions. Some examples of archetypal images include a Fool, a Magician, a Sphinx or a Witch or any of the other images of people on the Tarot cards, or images such as the Tower or Death.

Archetypal images are communicated from the levels of the Universe at which all consciousness is interconnected.

Geometric symbols: religious geometric symbols are also common. They may be Christian, Buddhist, Egyptian or other symbols. Examples of these are a cross, Star of David, ankh, Christ, Thoth or Buddha figure, or angelic images.

A Star of David   **An ankh**

Nature symbols: nature symbols such as flowers, trees, animals or birds frequently occur as messages in dreams, meditations, trance and clairvoyance. The meanings of many of these are derived from cultural and religious traditions. For example, a tree may occur frequently in Kabbalistic links because the Tree of Life is the central image of the Kabbalah. An ibis is a sacred Egyptian and hermetic symbol meaning wisdom. Eagles equate to freedom. Dogs can occur as a cosmic joke – as dog is an anagram of the word God. A dove commonly represents peace.

Elements: fire and water may occur in visions. Water is generally a symbol of emotion. Pay attention to the form in which it occurs. Fire is a cleansing, purifying and cathartic force. You may see it or feel its heat in another person or yourself.

A sphinx symbol

Symbols through the other senses: auditory images may include extracts of music or melodies as well as voices. Again, archetypal images may be picked up through this sense through angelic choirs, violins or chanting. Feelings such as warmth, and weightlessness or waves of tingling energy may come through clairsentience.

A nature symbol

PSYCHOMETRY

Psychometry is a skill by which a psychic reads an object by touch. In handling the object, the psychic can pick up events or emotions or details about people connected with the object. Many psychics will start off a reading by asking for an object belonging to the sitter so that they can tune in to their personal vibration.

How does psychometry work?

When you touch something, you leave an energy pattern or psychic imprint on it. It is as though you are leaving a magnetic recording directly on a tape. The stronger the emotions of the person handling the object, the clearer the imprint or signature that is left.

By holding the object and tuning in through your extrasensory perceptions, you can begin to pick up these subtle vibrations.

What objects can be used?

See if you can get hold of a personal object like a watch or a piece of jewellery, such as a necklace or a ring. Something that is used or worn frequently by its owner will maintain more of their vibration. The person whose belonging you are reading does not have to be present or alive. A photograph of a person will contain that person's vibrations and it is one of the best objects through which you can create a psychic link.

Be aware that everyone who touched an object will leave their pattern on it. Be careful of inherited jewellery, especially if it contains gem stones and crystals, which pick up magnetic imprints very easily. You will need to distinguish the different patterns belonging to different family members or you may end up picking up lots of information that is not relevant to the sitter.

How to practise psychometry exercise

1 Ask a friend for an object that belongs to them.

2 Sit and relax. Tune into your alpha state.

3 Hold the object in one hand and cup it with the other hand.

4 See what images begin to enter your mind. Don't judge them or worry about them making sense.

5 Say aloud what has come into your mind. The more you practise, the more confident you will become at voicing thoughts, even if they don't make immediate sense. You can ask your friend questions to confirm what you are thinking but it is better to ask yes/no

questions rather than open questions that might give you too much information and steer you away from your intuition.

A famous psychometrist

A famous psychometrist Gerald Croiset (1909–1980) was a psychic born in Holland. In 1949, he was asked by the police to comment on the impressions he received from a sealed box. He was able to tell them not only that the box contained a blood-stained shoe, but also that its owner was a girl who had been killed by a murderer by the name of Stevens. His description of the crime scene was confirmed by the police who were holding a man called Stevenson for the killing. Croiset went on to help the police with many other crimes. Psychometry is still used for some cases by the police, although often unofficially.

DOWSING

Dowsing can help to find objects, to heal, to find energy blocks in a home or to locate people. Most dowsers use dowsing rods or pendulums. Dowsing, also known as radioesthesia, has a history of about 7,000 years. Rods were used in Ancient Egypt and China. In the Middle Ages, dowsing was used to find coal in Europe. Dowsing has also been used widely to locate water underground.

Dowsing Rods

Two rods are used. They form an L shape and are traditionally made of copper or wood. You can make your own rods out of bent coat hangers. Cut the wires at the bottom. Bend each wire into a 90 degree angle

Dowsing rods

so that one side is shorter than another. Use the short side as the handle and the other side as the pointer.

How to use dowsing rods exercise

1 Hold one rod in each hand so that they are parallel to each other. Point them in one direction. Be sure the rod is horizontal to the ground.

2 You can hold them over a map or a physical location. If you are looking for water, for example, keep the idea of water in your mind as you walk in one direction.

3 When the rods cross you have found what you are looking for.

Dowsing a person's energy field exercise

1 At a distance of a few feet, face the person with your dowsing rods parallel to the ground.

2 State in your mind that you are measuring the boundaries of the person's energy field (aura). Focus only on this as you walk towards him or her.

3 Ask the person to remove any jewellery. Crystals and gemstones can affect the dowsing rods.

4 As you touch the energy field, the rods will cross.

Pendulums

You can make or buy a pendulum for psychic work. The ideal length is around six inches. Pendulums can be made of crystal, metal or any other material. If you don't have a pendulum, you can use a pendant on a chain.

Preparing your pendulum exercise

1 Hold the pendulum in front of you with your arm relaxed and solid. To start, you need to tune your pendulum into your energy. Ask the pendulum to give you a yes. The pendulum may swing in a particular direction or make a circular movement, for example clockwise. If you want to be clear, you may ask the pendulum to swing from front to back to indicate yes.

2 Next, ask the pendulum to swing in an opposite direction to indicate no. It may swing for example from side to side or anti-clockwise. Again, you can suggest to the pendulum that it chooses a particular direction to swing in.

3 You can use a pendulum chart to tune the pendulum in.

Preparing a pendulum

Using a pendulum to dowse for a missing object exercise

1 Ask a friend to hide an object for you.

2 Hold the pendulum over a map of the place or as you walk along the physical location.

3 Clear your mind of any distractions. Focus on what you wish to locate. Ask the pendulum to show you where the object is and to give you a yes signal when you have reached its location.

4 Ask the pendulum to give you a yes response when you locate what you are looking for.

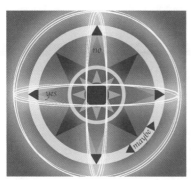

Pendulum chart

ASTRAL PROJECTION

Astral projection is when you have an 'out of body' experience – the experience of floating up so that you look down on your body. This reportedly happens during meditation, lucid dreaming or during a near-death experience. The soul moves around the astral plane in its astral body, linked to the physical body by a silver etheric umbilical cord.

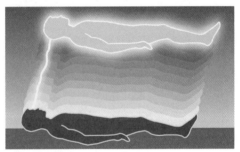

Astral projection

Astral travel

Some people claim to be able to travel far afield in their astral bodies; to different countries or even other planets. Others say they are able to communicate with other astral projectors during this state.

Evidence

The first study for astral travel was given by Frederik van Eeden (1860–1932) to the Society of Psychical Research at the beginning of the twentieth century. He told of his lucid dream experiences accompanied by dreams of flying. Since then, the Monroe Institute's Robert Monroe (1915–1995) has published many accounts of his experiences.

How to astral travel exercise

1 Attach a piece of rope or cord to the ceiling above you, so that it hangs down and you can touch it easily.

2 Imagine being able to reach out and touch it when your eyes are closed.

3 Now, relax and take yourself into the alpha state. Ask your spirit guide to stay with you and guide you during this experience. Surround yourself in white light.

4 Imagine in your mind's eye reaching out with your hands to the rope and pulling yourself up it hand over hand. Feel how the rope is to your touch. You will feel a tug to your etheric body. This can be felt either as a sharp pull or as pressure.

5 As your etheric body is pulled up, you will feel pressure and sometimes a slight dizziness. The feeling

of heaviness and dizziness, even vertigo, may intensify as you climb higher. Expect your trance state to deepen as this happens.

6 Your chakras now open up as you continue up the rope. Then your body begins to vibrate.

7 Finally, feel the sensation of becoming free of your physical body. You are floating above your body. Notice that you are looking down on your physical body to which you are still attached by a silver cord.

8 To travel forward or back, imagine that there is a magnet in front of you. It can pull you towards it, first with just a slight movement and then with a stronger and stronger pull.

9 To come back to your body, ask your spirit guide to help you. Notice the cord that connects you to your physical body. Imagine that your body is like a magnet and is drawing you back in. Float back down and back into your body.

10 When the two bodies connect again you may sometimes feel a bump.

11 Make sure you are fully in your body by grounding

yourself: imagine two roots coming out of your feet and growing deep into the ground right down to the earth's core. Close your chakras. Visualise drawing a silver line under your feet and up and round your head so that it makes a circle around you. When you feel fully present, open your eyes.

Remote viewing exercise

Remote viewing is being able to 'view' a place or object that is hidden from the viewer or at a distance. In remote viewing experiments, the viewer may be 'blind' to the target, in other words, not told what the target is. This is an area that has attracted a great deal of experiments. One of the most famous remote viewers is a former US Army intelligence officer, Joseph McMoneagle. The International Remote Viewing Association (IRVA) is a non-profit organisation that provides information about remote viewing and remote viewing experiments.

This exercise takes around five to ten minutes.

1 Ask a friend to select several photographs without showing them to you and put them in an envelope. Preferably, each image should be as different as possible with clear features.

2 Make sure you have paper and pens in front of you.

3 Relax, close your eyes, take several deep breaths and go to your alpha state.

4 Take each sealed envelope in turn.

5 Imagine that you can see through the envelope.

6 What impressions do you have? Start to sketch any impressions that come through. These impressions are likely to be fuzzy, half-clear images.

7 Notice, shapes and lines, colours, smells, sounds, textures, or tastes.

8 The key is to be prepared to take a risk. Even if something you see appears illogical, draw it anyway. This is often the piece of information that is most accurate. This way you will learn to distinguish psychic images from mental clutter. It does not matter if what you sketch makes any sense to you at the time. It may well make sense afterwards.

9 Number the drawing and proceed to the next one.

10 Show your friend your drawings. Make sure that you are objective about how successfully your remote viewing has been. Learn what was mental clutter and what was a clairvoyant image.

TELEKINESIS

Telekinesis, also known as psychokinesis is the ability to move objects, throw balls of energy or bend objects with the mind. One theory is that waves of magnetic energy created by intentional thought are forceful enough to push or pull an object.

How to practise telekinesis exercise

At first, practise at least once a day for about 15 minutes. Play with different objects and have fun.

1 Place an object such as a piece of paper or pen in front of you.

2 Imagine your body is filled with energy.

3 Focus your eyes on the object.

4 Close your eyes. Enter your alpha state.
Now visualise the object in front of you.

5 Imagine your energy and the energy of the object are blending together.

6 Focus your mind on moving the object away from you.

7 Focus your mind on moving the object towards you.

8 Focus your mind on moving the object to the left side.

9 Focus your mind on moving the object to the right side.

10 Open your eyes. Repeat the exercise more than once. Change the object if necessary.

Blocks

Even a tiny bit of doubt will block you from achieving positive results. Clear your mind of all doubt. Believe you can do it and you will.

Making an energy ball

Making an energy ball exercise

1 Hold out your hands so they are parallel to each other in front of you. Close your eyes. Relax.

2 Focus on the space between your hands. Visualise a ball of energy between your hands. Feel it growing stronger and stronger.

3 Moving your hands slightly back and forth will help you to find the outer edges of the ball.

Spoon-bending exercise

Spoon-bending became a focus of interest when Uri Geller, an Israeli-born practitoner of telekinesis showed his spoon-bending prowess on television worldwide in the 1970s.

You too can learn to bend a spoon without using any force other than mind power. The key to spoon bending is not to force the spoon to bend. Just allow it to happen: give permission to the spoon to bend.

1 Take a spoon or fork. Hold it in one or both hands.

2 Close your eyes. Relax.

3 Empty your mind. Simply focus on the object in front of you.

4 Slowly rub your fingers softly over the object. As you do this, feel the essence of the object: imagine you can feel right through the surface at its energetic level – the level of the very atoms that make it up.

5 Allow your energy to blend with the energy of the object. When you reach this point, the object will begin to bend.

Moving a compass exercise

For this exercise, always buy a cheap compass. As soon as you have succeeded in moving the compass, its energy structure will be permanently changed and you won't be able to use it again as a compass.

1 Put a compass on a flat surface in front of you.

2 Relax and enter your alpha state.

3 Put one of your hands about an inch above the compass.

4 Imagine your energy and the energy of the compass blending together.

5 Focus on moving the needle of the compass in a clockwise direction.

Directing a candle flame exercise

1 Meditate for a while so that you start the exercise in an alpha state.

2 Light a candle in front of you.

3 Focus on the flame of the candle. Clear your mind of other thoughts. Only see the flame. Let the candle, the surface it rests on and all objects around it fade out of your awareness.

4 Let your energy blend with the candle flame.

5 Stretch the flame upwards with your mind so that it grows taller and taller.

6 Now shrink the flame downwards so that it becomes smaller and smaller.

7 Play with the flame. Make it dance, bend, grow and shrink.

PRACTICAL TECHNIQUES

You can use your psychic powers for simple practical techniques to make your life easier as long as you are not harming others.

Problem solving exercise

1 With your eyes closed, relax and go to your alpha state.

2 Imagine there is a screen in front of you.

3 Project the problem situation on to the screen. View it briefly and then delete it. Say to yourself 'My problem is now in the past'.

4 Now imagine on your screen a road leading to a solution. Ask to be guided along the road. In your mind's eye see yourself walking along the road and as you do so a solution will soon present itself to you. See it clearly and say to yourself. 'Thank you for this solution now being realised.'

5 Now let go, knowing and trusting that your solution has already been put in place. Say to yourself: 'I now hand this matter over to the Universe.'

6 Every time you think of this matter in future, only think of the solution.

Problem-solving dream exercise

1 Before you go to sleep, relax and go to your alpha state.

2 Make sure that you have put a piece of paper and a pen by your bed so that you can write down any messages you have received in your dream in the morning when you wake up.

3 Imagine there is a screen in front of you just a little above eye level.

4 Briefly project the issue on to the screen. State inwardly, 'Tonight I ask for a dream that will help me to solve this issue. I will remember the information I am given in the dream when I wake up'.

5 Clear the screen. Visualise that there is a now a blank screen in front of you on which to project the answers that will come as you dream.

6 Let yourself drift off to sleep.

7 When you wake up in the morning, focus on your awareness of solving the problem. Write down any

messages or symbols that you have received. If there are any features of your dream that you don't understand straight away, write them down and ask your unconscious to give you an interpretation when the time is right.

Creating the future you want

Remember:

1 The Universe will always give you what you ask for. Every thought you have is like a prayer to the Universe. The Universe does not distinguish between positive, negative or unintentional thoughts.

2 There is a time delay between what you ask for and what you receive. However, just because you can't see what is happening, it doesn't mean nothing is happening. So always trust that your prayer has been answered.

3 The more emotion you direct towards your thoughts, the greater your desire, the greater your attention, the more likely you will choose this reality to manifest rather than another.

4 To create your future, first define a clear vision of what you want. Next believe that you already have it. If you keep your goals at the 'want' stage they will always remain a pace away. If you thank the

Universe as if they have already been realised, they will be, because you will have created a memory in your future. In other words, the energy is already manifesting in another dimension.

Creating your future exercise

1 Take a piece of paper and divide it into several sections. Label each segment as an area of your life. For example, relationships, money, career, social life, friendships, family, health, spiritual development. In each section write a goal that you have. These can be long-term, short-term, big or small goals. It doesn't matter how many goals you have – whether one, or 100. Describe each goal in as much detail as you can. Give each goal a summary title that is easy for you to remember. For example, 'house in country' or 'advanced skier'. Write these titles into each of your segments.

2 Read through your goals so that they are clear in your mind.

3 Are these goals in line with your spiritual purpose? Use your intuition. Check that each of your goals is good, not only for you, but for the rest of the world as well. If your instinct tells you to make adjustments, do so.

4 Now close your eyes. Take a few deep breaths and

take yourself to your alpha state. Visualise a screen in front of you just above your eye level.

5 Project each goal in turn onto the screen. See yourself realising the goal. You may also project onto the screen scenes of your life when you have realised all these goals.

6 Make sure you involve all your senses in the visualisation. Imagine the colours, scents and sounds of the pictures. The more detail you can sense, the easier it is for you to draw in energy from higher levels to manifest the goals accurately.

7 Thank the cosmos for already having made these goals a reality. Hand the goals over to the higher powers in the Universe knowing that they will be realised. Letting go with certainty is a very important part of the process.

8 Keep your list of goals safe. If you have an altar in your home, put them on the altar.

9 Revisit your goals each day for four weeks. Direct energy into your goals through your attention to them.

10 At the end of a month put the goals away and revisit them every few weeks until they are realised.

Improving your skills exercise

1 Close your eyes, relax and go to your alpha state.

2 Project a screen in front of you just above eye level.

3 Visualise yourself doing the skill you want to improve. For example, maybe you want to play golf, or ski better or be effective in presenting to an audience.

4 See yourself doing the skill in a relaxed and competent way.

5 If you know someone who already has this skill, you can visualise them in front of you. Step into their body and feel yourself practising the skill in the way that they do it. Ask yourself to remember how you did the skill in this way and come back to your own body.

6 Say thank you in advance to the Universe. State: 'I am now at the best level of this skill that I am capable of.'

GIVING A READING

Friends – or as you develop, clients – may come to you and ask for a general reading.

1 First make sure you are seated comfortably.

2 Create a comfortable environment for you and the sitter. Make sure you are sitting in a clear space in which you feel calm. Clear your mind of all distractions. Take a few deep breaths. Go to your alpha state.

3 Draw your attention in to a point of focus. If the person sitting in front of you has come to you with a particular issue, focus your attention on this issue. If the person is asking for general feedback, simply ask inwardly for guidance for the sitter.

4 Relax and let information enter into your mind. This may come in the form of feelings, visual images or other sensations.

5 State what you receive. Be careful not to distort the information with too much interpretation or to lead the sitter into giving you too much information. For example, if you see an image of a car, just say, 'I see a car' – not 'Do you have a car?'

6 Don't let your conscious mind censor the information you get. Say it even if it sounds ridiculous.

7 If you are not getting much information, ask yourself some other questions around the subject. For example, 'What information would be helpful in relation to this issue?'

Difficult information

What happens if you receive a piece of information that seems to point to a death or illness of someone connected with the sitter? Some mediums and psychics will not give this information. Others will state the message exactly as it is received so that the sitter can take action to change the situation. Use your intuition. Ask yourself, 'What is the best way I can give this information that is to the highest good of all concerned?' Remember, whatever you decide to say, your role is to help the sitter not to prove your abilities.

SPIRIT GUIDES

WHAT ARE SPIRIT GUIDES?

Your spirit guides are energies or beings of light that live within the invisible Universe. Just as you are a being who has a certain vibration or frequency, spirit guides exist at faster vibrations on the higher planes. Because they have no physical bodies, they can travel between dimensions.

Some cultures see guides as a wise aspect of our higher self. Other traditions see guides as spiritual entities – evolved, or evolving, independent beings who we can call upon for help. They believe that some spirit guides are beings who have been alive on the earth and now want to help those left behind. Other guides have not been incarnated (experienced a physical life).

A spirit guide is a benevolent force. They are there to help you according to your best and highest interests, to teach you spiritual truths. Because they are outside the physical world, they are not constrained by its rules of time or space and can always be there when you call on them.

If a dead relative appears as a spirit guide to you, it is because they have become developed in spiritual ways, and your close bond of love allows them to come to you and work with you.

How spirit guides manifest

Spirit guides can choose to appear to you telepathically, by speaking to you inside your head, or visually – in a form that is familiar to you – as a human or as an animal.

They do not appear in their true 'light' form as the human brain finds it easier to communicate with something it recognises – usually a form from this physical existence.

Generally, the spirits 'clothe' themselves in a form either they have had when they were in the physical world or that will be recognised as an archetype, for example, an angel. The form will remain consistent so that you will recognise the spirit as the same guide when it reappears. Spirits you knew in the physical world tend to appear in a form that you will be able to identify easily, for example at the age they were when they died.

What do spirit guides do?

A spirit guide will give you wise guidance and insight. It is up to you when to contact your guides. Remember that all guidance is freely given, and will always be available without judgement. You are free to work with more than one spirit guide at a time.

Issues guides can help with

Guides can provide help for you or another person in several ways:

- Physical, emotional, mental and spiritual healing.
- For advice about major life decisions and general self-development.
- To contact a deceased loved one to let a bereaved relative know they are okay.
- To open up your creative channels.
- For astral travel.
- For divination.
- Bringing together soulmates.
- Experiencing past lives.
- Finding your spiritual mission and life purpose.

Free will

Under cosmic law, a spirit guide cannot take over your life. If you hit a rough spot and need help, you must ask them for it. They won't automatically interfere, and a spirit guide cannot force you to listen. Nor will working with a guide absolve you from making your own decisions about your life. Because you have free will and choice, you can choose to ignore or act upon this guidance. You may also ask a guide to leave at any time.

A trained medium will often work with one guide (a doorkeeper) to help them contact other spirits.

This guide may stay with them for their lifetime or come for a few days, weeks or years to help around a particular issue before disappearing.

You don't have to have any psychic powers to have a guide. We each have at least one guardian spirit who will stay with us for our entire life. However, a medium will use guides specifically to link in with the spirit world.

You may call upon a number of guides for different purposes as long as they are for good. You do not have to know in advance the name of a guide you are calling. Just state what kind of help you need and ask for a guide.

You can ask for guidance from a particular person who is now in spirit. If you have a strong affinity with that person they may contact you and offer help.

Use your guide for positive purposes and treat him as your partner. You do not need to pay him, except in choosing to be of service to the world in whatever way is appropriate for you. Your guides will see that as an appropriate payment.

TYPES OF SPIRIT GUIDES

Different traditions refer to and train contact with different types of spirit guides. Here are some of the main types:

Guardian angels

A guardian (angel) is a highly enlightened spirit who helps us as an individual. They are there throughout your life and will help you with your soul/spiritual purpose. They know everything that happens to you in this lifetime and any previous lifetimes, and are at your death and transition into the afterlife.

When you have an instinct that you should do something, it may be your guardian giving you a push in the right direction. However, you always have free will: you can choose to ignore your gut reaction.

Relations, friends, ancestors and soul families

Our loved ones who have died are not with us all the time, but will come to us when needed to give advice. We are linked to them through love and a common purpose. Families have chosen to be together as souls because of a need of each member to experience a particular aspect of him or herself and to evolve through the group connection.

Helpers

Guides have knowledge of the other realms that you need as a psychic. A helper is a guide who can be called on to teach you, and help you to develop a particular aspect of your life or psychic talent that they are interested in. An example would be a guide who when alive was a doctor. Even if you don't have any medical ability, they can guide you and give you healing abilities.

Doorkeepers

Doorkeeper guides protect you from negative energies as you explore the spiritual realms through mediumship or channelling. These guides will make sure that you avoid the influence of negative spirits.

How to contact your spirit guide

Contact with your spirit guide can happen as soon as you learn to tune into the higher frequencies or vibrations. The more you awaken your psychic abilities through regular meditation and focus, the more attuned you will become to other dimensions and the spirits that live in them.

It's a bit like switching TV or radio channels which is why the communication is sometimes called channelling. The connection is usually made through telepathy: the guides speak to you inside your head. They may also choose to communicate through dreams, meditation or while you are in a relaxed state writing, painting, dancing or playing music.

Making their presence known

A guide may also choose to move an object to alert you to its presence or even appear in a visual form as a person or animal, as ectoplasm or as a shape in a photograph.

Dreamtime is another place where your guides may visit you. In dreamtime we raise our vibrations and can link up more easily with the higher spheres. When you dream, your higher self communicates with your guides and receives any messages it needs to store in your unconscious.

Trance communication

Some guides will speak through their mediums in trance communication or help other spirits to come through the physical voice of the medium.

A famous example of this was the guide **Silver Birch** who spoke through the medium Maurice Barbanell (1902–1981) a trance medium, journalist and the founder, in 1932, of Psychic News, a weekly newspaper devoted to psychic matters. He published many books including nine volumes of channelled teachings by his guide, who is believed to have lived thousands of years previously.

Synchronicity

Guides can create synchronicities in your life to draw your attention to particular events or situations. A synchronicity is a seemingly accidental occurrence – for example, a chance meeting with someone from the past you have just been thinking about, or finding money lying on the ground just when you needed it.

Synchronicities can happen because the physical rules of time and space are ignored. Because your guides live in a higher dimension without physical rules, they can cause events to happen at this level that then manifest in our physical world. The purpose of synchronicities is to alert us to things that are happening in our life that we need to be aware of as part of our soul's development. If, for example, you meet someone in extraordinary happenstances, it is because your souls need you to meet, even if the reason is not always immediately obvious.

Talking to your spirit guides

Have a set time where you focus on communicating with your spirit guides.

Prepare your space: To begin any exercise, sit in a comfortable position and relax with your eyes closed and your legs uncrossed. Make sure it is a position you can maintain for about 30 minutes.

Create a peaceful and calm environment in which to sit. You may want to burn incense, light candles or play relaxing music. You can also make a small altar or bring sacred objects into your space.

State your intent: Begin by asking for protection. State that your intention is to meet your guide and to receive guidance. Ask that all that happens during this meditation is for your highest good. State that your intent is that only 'beings of light' enter your space. You can do this in your mind or aloud.

White light: Take a deep breath. Open up your chakras and imagine that white light is coming down from the Universe. It enters through your heart and fills up your entire body. State that the white light of protection will protect you against any negative energies. Imagine any worries, tensions or stress leaving your body.

Contacting your spirit guide exercise

1 State your intention. Invite your guide or guides to come to you. Ask for God or the God-energy to stay with you on this journey.

2 With your eyes closed, look up towards the third eye, located between your two brows at the pineal gland.

3 Now imagine that there is a beautiful tranquil place in which you feel totally relaxed. See what comes into your mind instinctively. It could be a hillside or a garden. Wherever you choose, this will be the same place in which you contact your guide in future. Imagine that you are walking through this place. Feel it with your senses.

4 You may feel a pressure on the top of your head as your crown chakra opens up, or sensations on one side of your body.

5 There is a mist in front of you. Your guide is waiting for you behind the mist. Ask for your guide to appear to you. Become aware that your guide is approaching you.

6 Ask for the mist to clear and for your guide to be revealed to you. Ask to see your guide's clothing and shape.
   Your guide may appear in a visual image or may come through in thoughts and feelings first of all.

Strengthening your link with your spirit guide

7 As you become more familiar with your guide you will feel their energy clearly entering your presence, so that you will recognise any differences from other guides who may come through in the future.

8 Greet your guide. First, ask for their name. Ask for any special guidance they have for you at this point. You may come back and ask further questions in future. If you wish to, invite your guide to stay with you to perform a particular purpose, to stay with you on a daily basis, or to reconnect with you in your dreams.

9 When you have finished, thank your guide with love. Watch your guide leave you and go back into the mist.

10 Imagine yourself coming back to now, still swathed in white light.

11 Become aware of your surroundings. Finally close down your chakras by imagining each one closing into a tight bud like the bud of a lotus flower.

12 Finally, imagine roots coming down into the ground from your feet so you are firmly rooted back in physical reality. It is always important to make sure that you are fully 'back to earth' before carrying on with your daily life.

Questions for your guide

Try to ask questions that can be answered with a simple 'yes' or 'no' or other short answer. Ask each question once and wait for the answer. Don't try to test or trick your guide. For example,

- What is your name?
- May I call you by this name?
- Can I ask you questions now?
- What is your connection to me?
- What is your function?
- How many guides do I have?
- I would like to meet a guide who will help me with my question today. Please ask a guide who can help me with my question to come to me now.
- How can I best be of service in this lifetime?
- Am I working in accordance with my spiritual path and higher purpose?
- Will you guide me in the next phase of my spiritual journey?
- Is there any karma I need to resolve to develop further?
- Should I be working as a medium? Clairvoyant? Healer?
- Do I need to meditate more?
- Do I need to be with other people to develop my psychic abilities?
- Can you help me with my creative project?
- Can you help me to contact (name)?
- Can you give me a message from (name)?

Identifying your guides

You may not see your guides straightaway in a recognisable form. They may appear first as lights or a feeling of tingling, or even a brush of feathers on the back of your neck. When you sense clairvoyantly or clairsentiently that a guide is present, ask him to identify itself in a form that is recognisable to you. Gradually, you will make sense of what you see and feel and be able to identify the guide next time he appears.

Names

Not every guide will give you their name. They may prefer to be identified by a symbol, shape, sound or smell.

Ways guides identify themselves

- A scent, particularly one that has associations or memories for you.
- A sound, for example a bell or chime.
- A feeling, such as a tickle, a hand touching you, the brush of wings on your shoulders, tingling in your arm.

Contacting your guide in your dreams exercise

1 Set up your room before you go to sleep by burning some lavender to calm and clear the energy in the room.

2 Take several deep breaths. Relax into your alpha state.

3 State clearly in your mind: 'I am open to meeting my spirit guide(s) and communicating with them. I ask them to come to me in my dreams tonight. I will remember these dreams when I awake tomorrow morning.'

4 Make sure you have a notebook by your bed ready to record what you dream.

5 Allow yourself to drift off to sleep.

6 Record what happens. Repeat this exercise on consecutive nights until you establish clear communication.

Psychic Art

Psychic artists are mediums who draw pictures of spirits, usually for a sitter who is a relative. They may also draw pictures of spirit guides. Many of the artists have no particular talent for art, but allow the spirit guides to work through their bodies to produce the drawings.

OTHER GUIDES

Angels, archangels

Angels and archangels can act as guides but differ in several respects from other spirit guides.

The four main archangels

Archangel	Description	Direction governed
Uriel	'God's light', 'Pillar of fire'. Brought alchemy to man	North
Michael	'He who looks like God'. Warrior angel, archangel of the light and the sun	South
Raphael	'God Heals', Healer angel	East
Gabriel	'God is my strength', Spirit of truth	West

The first is that they are on a different plane of evolution from spirits who have had past lives on earth. Unlike other spirits, an angel can appear in a human form or other physical manifestation.

The second is that an angel will come to you and help you even if you don't ask. Angels, unlike other guides, appear to be watching out for our interests

Associated Colours	Helps
Rich fiery red	Change, writing, transforming emotions, finding spiritual path, natural disasters
Gold	Illumination, overcoming obstacles, courage, self-esteem, protection, life purpose, light-workers
Yellow	Healing for humans and animals, addictions, space clearing, spirit release, travel, protection of children
Silver	Safe travel, removes sorrow and regrets, adoption, conception, fertility, writing, art

all the time. They are guardians rather than teachers or helpers to those on earth.

An archangel is a higher level of angel. You can light candles to the archangels to ask them for help in the areas they govern, or for general protection in your spirit guide contact.

How to form a protective circle for any spirit work

Light a white candle in the space you are working, in each of the compass directions. Call upon the name of the archangel for protection (see table below), starting in the East. When you have finished your work, blow out the candles starting with the candle positioned to the North, and move round the compass directions: North, East, South, West.

Invocations (prayer for help)

Write your prayer on a piece of paper. State the name of the angel or archangel you are asking for help. State the prayer three times. Thank them for their divine intervention.

Saints, sages and the great white brotherhood

Saints and sages such as Confucius or the Virgin Mary can help in the same way as angels. In addition, you can call on help from the great white brotherhood – those on the highest planes who look after the spiritual direction of all those on earth.

NATURE GUIDES

Animal guides

The Celtic and American shamanistic traditions use power animals and spirit animals as guides. These are animals in spirit form that come to you to help. They have a similar function to other spirit guides. Different traditions attribute qualities to each animal. If you feel a strong affinity to an animal, it is important to look up archetypal qualities or to go by your instinct as to what support the animal is giving to you.

Nature spirits

Elementals are spirits or etheric thought forms that represent an element: earth, fire, water, air. Elementals appear as a colour or are felt as a wave of energy. Devas are the higher level of nature spirits. They act as sacred guardians for whole areas. For example, if an earth elemental helps a seed, a deva looks after the whole garden.

Main types of elementals

Earth

Gnomes – Create form from a spark of consciousness, for example, to turn a seed into a plant. They are said to live for a thousand years. Include: **Brownies, Pixies, Elves, Pygmies, Satyrs, Pans, Leprechauns, Nymphs, Tree spirits**

Water

Undines – Live in water in a shape resembling human form. They work with vital essences and liquids in nature and people. Include: **Naiads, Mermaids, Ocenids, Water sprites, Oreads**

Air

Sylphs – Live at the tops of mountains and high buildings. It is said they may assume human form and are drawn to help creative people. Include: **Fairies, Light elves, Sprites, Mountain spirits, Hill trolls**

Fire

Salamanders – Fire elementals that appear as balls of light or in lizard-like form. You cannot light a fire without a salamander being present. Include: **Jinn, Djinn, Dragons, Fairies, Will-o'-the-wisps, Earth lights**

Contacting a nature spirit

Sit quietly in nature and open up your chakras. Listen in alpha state for any messages that come to you. When you finish leave an offering for the deva and elemental relating to the appropriate element.

Offerings

Element	Colours	Crystals	Other offerings
Earth	Green or brown	Agates, emeralds, rose quartz, tiger's eye, malachite	Flowers, honey, beer, nuts, seeds, salt, soil, fruit, scent of geranium, cypress, vervain or patchouli
Water	Silver or blue	Coral, jade, opal, aquamarine, pearl, tourmaline, fluorite	Shells, nets, silver, copper, milk, scent of thyme, jasmine, lemon
Air	Yellow or grey	Turquoise, amethyst, citrine, sapphire, sodalite, citrine, clear quartz	Wind chimes, feathers, scents such as lavender or lemon grass
Fire	Red, gold or orange	Ruby, carnelian, amber, hematite, bloodstone, obsidian	Lights, orange fruit, gold, scents of basil, chamomile, juniper, lime, cloves, orange, cinnamon

DIVINATION

SEEING YOUR FUTURE

In the psychic Universe, your potential future already exists. It is the effect of your past decisions that you made both before and after your birth. According to this thinking, you knew why you were incarnated before you were born. As soon as you are born, you have free will to make mistakes and take actions and to change or fulfill your destiny. Your higher self is aware of your future as it evolves.

Prophecy and divination

Prophecy has historically played an important part in many cultures, including the Celts, Druids, Greeks, Chinese, Native Americans, Egyptians and Hindus. Many prophecies in ancient cultures were based on divination – the attempt to communicate with supernatural entities and to interpret omens through various methods such as oracles, cloud formations or the reading of tea leaves.

Divination is a way of asking questions of your higher self about your future. You can ask questions about big life-changing decisions or a specific area that requires immediate attention.

Personal divination exercise

You will need a recording device: a minidisc player or tape recorder.

1 Decide what question you want to ask.

2 Sit down in a place where you will not be disturbed, and make sure the recording device is in a position where it can pick up your voice. Press the record button.

3 Close your eyes. Take a few deep breaths and go into your alpha state.

4 As soon as you reach this altered state of consciousness, begin to speak out loud. Just say whatever comes into your head. Don't stop, analyse, try to understand, or worry about what you say.

5 Stop when it feels natural. Come back to your full awareness of your body. Open your eyes.

6 Play back what has been recorded. Notice any words or thoughts that stand out or relate to your question.

7 Practise this regularly.

Automatic writing exercise

Automatic writing is a method by which you can channel messages the spirits want to give to you. Not everybody has a gift for this. However, do the exercise a few times and see what results. You will need paper and a pen for this exercise.

1 Place the paper in front of you.

2 Hold the pen in your writing hand. However, hold it very loosely.

3 Relax and go to your alpha state with your eyes open.

4 Allow the pen to begin to move across the paper. Let go of conscious control.

5 Just let whatever shapes or letters form in front of you.

6 The first time you do this, writing or images may form on the paper or what appears may be indecipherable. Let what happens happen.

7 Repeat the exercise on other occasions for about 15 minutes each time. See if you can interpret any of the images or words that are drawn.

DIVINATION TOOLS

Divination can be developed through the use of tools to help receive and decode visual symbols and develop inner sight. These include crystals, crystal balls, rune stones and cards.

Blessing your tools

Each time you use a tool, place one hand over it. Offer a blessing for the tool. State that you invite the God-energy to bless whatever work you intend

Divination tools

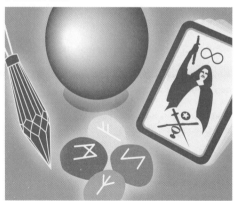

to do with the tool. Ask that what happens be for the highest good of those present, the world at large and in line with the highest spiritual purpose.

Book divination exercise

This is a very simple form of divination. You can use a dictionary or a sacred book such as the bible.

1 Place the book in front of you.

2 Close your eyes. Take a few deep breaths and go to your alpha state.

3 Ask a question out loud.

4 With your eyes still closed, focus on the question and hold the book in your hands. When you feel intuitively it is the right time, open the book at the page your hands guide you to.

5 Let your fingers rest on the page and guide you to a particular spot on the page.

6 Keep the spot marked and open your eyes.

7 What is marked at this point should relate to or answer the question you have asked.

CARTOMANCY

Many psychics use cards to tune into the higher vibrations. In cartomancy a psychic uses conventional playing cards as a tool on which to focus and make predictions for an individual or about a situation. 'Mancy' comes from the Greek word 'manteia', divination.

A visual prompt for divination helps you to tune in to the spirit world more effectively. You can develop particular meanings for an individual card from your intuition about its significance in a reading, or you can refer to one of the many books about card reading.

The Tarot

The Tarot is a deck of cards used for divination that developed during the fourteenth and fifteenth centuries. It consists of 78 cards and 4 suits. Twenty-two of the cards are illustrated trumps, known as the Major Arcana. The other 56 cards are known as the Minor Arcana.

'Arcana' means 'secret'. The word Tarot comes either from the Kabbalistic word 'Torah' – the sacred Jewish text, or more likely from a popular card game in Italy in the Middle Ages called 'Tarocco'.

The Hermetic Order of the Golden Dawn believed that the system and symbols of the Tarot encompassed

numerology, astrology and the Kabbalah, drawing
upon the magical and mystical knowledge of
Ancient Egypt, Persia, and the Jewish religion.

What cards should I use?

The Rider-Waite Pack is
the most well-known
Tarot deck. However,
any deck is perfectly
acceptable for
divination work. The
Thoth pack was
specifically developed
by Aleister Crowley
(1875–1947) for its
esoteric content and is
very powerful.

Although the
symbols are designed
to trigger images from
archetypal
consciousness,
ultimately it is your
interaction with the
cards that give them
power and energy.

The Magician

The Fool

How to use the Tarot for divination

Each Tarot card has an accepted meaning. The Major Arcana cards represent the major, sometimes karmic issues in the 'querant' or sitter's life. The Minor Arcana represent more day-to-day occurrences and incidents.

There are various spreads you can learn to read the Tarot, including the Celtic Cross. A simple starting point is to lay out a three-card spread:

Three-card spread divination exercise

1 Relax. Hold the pack in your left hand. Express your intention that the reading provide you with guidance about a particular question.

2 First, shuffle the pack. Although this seems random, because your intention is clear, when you shuffle, you invite the energy of the Universe to bring order to chaos.

3 Cut the cards with your left hand three times, and then put them together in one pile. Fan the cards out and ask the sitter to select three cards from the deck. Lay them out in a row. The card on the left represents the past, the card in the middle, the present, and the card on the right, the future.

4 Although the cards have particular meanings, you can also use your psychic skills to divine the

Picture of a three-card spread

relationships between the cards and particular meanings relating to the sitter.

5 The reading will always be general but with a context for the question you will be able to feel and interpret what is being shown to you.

Looking after your cards

Treat your cards with respect. Traditionally, you should wrap your Tarot cards in silk and store them in a special box. Many psychics prefer that other people do not touch their cards except to cut the deck during a reading, so that their personal link with the cards remains strong.

SCRYING

Scrying is a method of divination. The word scrying comes from the Old English word 'descry' and means 'to reveal'.

Scrying uses an object as a focus to clear the mind and to deepen trance states, overriding the conscious mind. Images and ideas are projected from the object into the mind of the scryer, who can then interpret them.

Types of scrying

The stereotypical image of scrying is a fortune teller with a crystal ball. In fact, scrying can use innumerable tools, including mirrors, sand, clouds and crystal balls, as objects to gain a clear vision about a person or situation. Any of the four elements (earth, air, water or fire) can also be used for scrying. In Western traditions, objects with a shiny surface are thought to be the best for visions.

History of scrying

Scrying has been around for thousands of years:

- **Ancient Egyptians:** Scrying was part of Ancient Egyptions' initiation rituals. They scryed with dark liquids including blood, as well as mirrors, water and oil. They were also adept at dream scrying. The Egyptian goddess Hathor is said to carry a shield that reflects the truth back to those who look at it.

- **Romans:** Romans used shiny objects and stones.
- **Ancient Greeks and Celts:** Greeks and Celts both scryed with polished quartz crystal, black glass, and water.
- **Nostradamus:** The sixteenth century prophet scryed using water.

Europe's most famous historical scryer was the alchemist **John Dee** (1527–1609), a London-born Elizabethan scientist and mathematician who devoted his life to divination, astrology, alchemy and magic. In 1582, with Edward Kelley (1555–1597), Dee sought to contact the angels using a scrying crystal. He claimed that the angels had dictated several books to him in an angelic (Enochian) language. The crystal ball that Dee and Kelley used was made of the black shiny crystal obsidian, and is on display in the British Museum in London.

Night-time scrying

Many diviners prefer to work at night. In particular, witches scry at night in magical circles. This prevents excessive interference from vibrations emanating from the hustle and bustle of daily life.

Crystal balls

Use a clear crystal ball made of natural quartz. Choose one with as few natural imperfections as possible. If in doubt, hold your hand over the ball and feel the vibration of the crystal – it should 'feel' right to you. It does not matter what size ball you use, though the bigger the crystal ball, theoretically the stronger the energy it should carry. It is also easier to see images in a bigger object.

Cleaning your crystal ball

Always clean a new crystal. You can do this by putting it in the sunlight and moonlight for 24 hours.

Mirrors

Mirrors were originally used for scrying as they were seen as being linked to the moon and as being a solid form of water. Any type of mirror can be used for divination, though round and oval mirrors are best. Some psychics say that old and silver framed mirrors are most effective.

Mirrors are supposed to have originated in Persia. They were used by the Magi for Catoptromancy – a form of divination. Historically in the West, scryers and alchemists preferred mirrors made of polished obsidian, shewstone, copper, brass, silver or made of a layer of glass covering mercury. In Rome, the scryers were known as Specularii. The ancient Chinese used metal concave mirrors.

Black mirrors

Traditional scryers may prefer using a black mirror. You can make a black mirror by painting the glass on the front of a mirror black. A black mirror ensures that when you look at it you do not see your own reflection.

Seeing past lives

Look at a mirror in a dark room with a torch placed just below your chin so that your face is slightly illuminated. Go to your alpha state. Look with your third eye through the mirror image. Your face may change and manifest in a form from a previous life.

Mirror messages

Spirits will sometimes leave messages on steamed up bathroom mirrors. These usually appear suddenly as pictures rather than words. Spirits treat mirrors as portals from the spirit world to the material world.

How to scry exercise

1 Sit with the scrying object or speculum (a type of mirror) in front of you. Bless the object.

2 Relax and take yourself into a meditative/alpha state. You can keep your eyes closed or open.

3 Be clear about what your intention is for this session.

4 Attune yourself to the object by focusing on it and allowing its energy to fill your being.

5 Ask for a message or vision about the situation or question you have in mind.

6 Look at the object with your third eye. Note what mental images or impressions appear. Allow time for this to happen.

7 Be aware that messages may come in symbolic form and need to be interpreted. For example, in a trance state you may notice that the imperfections in a crystal or the ripples in water begin to mean something to you.

OUIJA BOARDS

It is believed that the word Ouija comes from the French and German words for 'yes': 'oui' and 'ja'. Even though the term Ouija is a trademark for a talking board surrounded by letters and numbers, it is also a term in common usage to describe a board used to communicate with spirits. It is also called a spirit board or a talking board. This can be used by one or more users. Ouija boards are generally used as part of a séance.

Ouija boards

How a Ouija board works

The users of the board put one or more fingers on a planchette (a thin, heart-shaped piece of wood, mounted on castors) or glass in the centre of the board. They ask for the spirits to come in to offer guidance and ask a question. The planchette or glass is then moved outside the conscious control of the users around the board stopping at different letters to spell out a message. Users believe that a spirit controls the central object and communicates through it.

Messages

The messages that come through the board may make sense immediately, they may make no sense at all, or call for liberal interpretation from the participants. As with any tool you use as part of your psychic development, be cautious about the flavour and distortions you can put on what you receive.

The sceptical view

The sceptical view is that Ouija boards do in fact produce messages without conscious control of the board by one or more people. However, the users of the board are unconsciously using minute movements of their fingers to move the glass or planchette. These are known as ideomotor movements.

How easily a group can be convinced about the other worldly nature of the messages has been demonstrated on TV by illusionists such as Derren Brown and Penn and Teller.

Dangers of Ouija boards

Many people see using Ouija boards as a game, but if you believe in the spirit world you should be cautious in using them.

Other methods for contacting the spirits are safer than using a Ouija board.

The psychic Edward Cayce said that Ouija boards are dangerous. It is thought that inexperienced players can be tricked by 'harmful' or 'evil' spirits of low vibrations into doing their will. Some researchers into these phenomena believe that they can attribute cases of spiritual or 'demonic' possession to the use of Ouija boards. The Christian religion disapproves of Ouija boards, believing that they are used to contact evil spirits.

PSYCHIC POWERS IN THE HOME

Every building has its own energy. An empty home feels different from a home full of happy people, and different again from a home where an ill person lives. You may feel drawn to one house and immediately want to get out of another.

Certain buildings attract high levels of psychic activity. This may be positive – for example, a place where spiritual activity is used for good – or negative: a 'haunted' space.

This chapter looks at different paranormal activity in the home and the psychic powers you can use here.

Negative energy

Buildings

Having ill, addicted, mentally unstable or negative people in a home can leave a residual energy in the building. Negative energy is left when the physical structure or objects within a home have picked up vibrations because of the emotion that has accompanied events there. This process may take several years, or it may happen very quickly. Physical objects maintain a magnetic imprint or charge that psychics can pick up on. This is known as a psychic imprint or signature.

Objects

Objects such as furniture or ornaments can also pick up general negative energy. If these objects are not cleaned, the negative energy can block you from attracting positive situations and people into your life.

Psychic clearing

There are several levels of clearing. You can clear your home of energy yourself when, for example, you first move house, or when someone who is depressed or negative has visited you. However, to clear a stubborn ghost, it is best to call in an expert who regularly works in this area, such as a priest or shaman.

If you think your home is attracting unwanted energy, check what you know about the history of where you live. Make a note of anything that might have negative energy associated with it. For example, an orphanage or wartime hospice may have picked up karmic energy that needs to be released.

Who do you currently spend time with in your home? How much time do you spend with people who are fearful, full of anger and hatred or jealousy? Having happy experiences in the home will build its positive vibration.

Make sure you get rid of anything from your home that has bad associations for you or that has picked up harmful energy. For example,

1 Clutter and rubbish.

2 Objects and pictures that have bad memories for you, negative associations or that you simply find unattractive.

3 Dead plants.

4 Anything that has previously been owned by someone with negative energy or who has harmful thoughts towards you.

5 Books on black magic.

6 Books on subjects surrounded by hate such as racism.

7 Drugs.

Next:
1 Clean and dust.

2 Smudge your home with sage smoke. You can make your own bundles of sage or buy ready-made smudge sticks.

3 Use sounds such as Tingsha bells (Tibetan bells used in yoga and meditation), or purifying music

with a high vibration such as Gregorian chants or religious songs.

4 Burn incense such as rosewood or rose. Sandalwood is very effective when followed by frankincense. Waft the scents through the home, and ask for protection against negative energy from white light, angels and higher energies such as Christ or the Buddha.

5 Open the windows and let fresh air into the house.

6 Fill your home with pictures, plants, fresh flowers and objects that give you pleasure when you look at them.

7 Paint your home.

Second-hand goods

Some cultures won't touch second-hand objects because they are afraid of attracting another person's karma. Make sure you energetically clean anything that has already been used by someone else.

Clean objects with sage smoke and surround them with white light. Metal and crystal objects should be cleaned on several consecutive days.

Psychic protection in the home

You can put protection not only around yourself but also around your home and any objects you use regularly such as your car.

Just imagine placing a bubble of white light around the place, object and people associated with it. If you have an altar or meditation place in the home, make sure you put white light around it every day.

Sacred space

If you regularly practise your psychic work in a particular location but neglect to protect yourself you will leave yourself open to problems.

Create a sacred space in your home. This can be any space where you have control over who comes in and out. Bless the space with white light and a prayer of gratitude for what you learn and discover here. Build the energy here every day through your meditation work.

Shrines and altars

You can also set aside a small corner of your home for a shrine or altar. It doesn't have to be big, just a place where you can put meaningful objects such as candles, crystals, religious or mystical symbols such as pictures of angels and saints, paper on which you have written down your personal goals, or Tarot cards to bring in particular energies. You can burn incense here or use a special cloth to symbolise that this is a clean energy area.

Place a candle in a bowl of water on your altar. Light it to symbolize your safe passage through uncharted waters as you meditate or carry out psychic practices.

Shrines and altars

'HAUNTED' HOUSES

Poltergeists

The word 'poltergeist' comes from the German words for 'to knock' and 'rumbling spirit'. Poltergeists, unlike ghosts, enjoy being mischievous and may be violent.

Poltergeists are discarnate spirits which seem to be particularly drawn to houses where there is a child with emotional problems who is at the beginning of puberty – around 12 to 14 years old. The child is not generally aware of anything he or she is doing. However, if the child leaves the home the activity usually ceases. In some cases, poltergeist activity will follow the child from house to house.

Poltergeist activity

- Objects being moved around or thrown.
- Bed shaking.
- Thumping and knocking.
- People being levitated.

Why does it happen?

The poltergeist activity may be caused by unconscious psychokinesis (telekinesis) – that is the outward expression of internal psychological upset.

Changes in hormones and strong emotions inside a child's physical body create an outward charge that attracts the negative spirit.

Some believe poltergeists are 'magnetic imprints' or 'recordings' within the building's fabric. This happens when emotional energy has been very intense. Phenomena such as partly visible manifestations appear at intervals because the magnetic imprint keeps resetting itself like a tape on playback until the energy plays itself out.

History

Poltergeists go back to the time of ancient Rome and Egypt. Stories include stones raining on people, and are consistent with current accounts. The most famous fictional poltergeist is the one in the film of the same name.

Famous poltergeists

- 1877: the Bell witch.
- 1848: the Fox sisters haunting.
- 1967: the Risenheim poltergeist.
- 1977: the Enfield poltergeist.

GHOSTS

Ghosts are discarnate spirits who are confused or unwilling to go into the light and so are trapped between dimensions. If their souls are to evolve, ghosts need to be persuaded by an expert to move on and go to the light.

All ghosts have been alive on the earth at some point – whether as a human or an animal. Ghosts of people have the same personalities they had when they were alive.

Why ghosts haunt

- Sometimes ghosts do not know they are dead because the death came too quickly.
- They may be afraid of being punished when they go to the light because of how they lived during their physical life.
- They have unfinished business such as a message to give to a loved one or a message about violent circumstances surrounding their death.
- They want to remain near their family or the home they lived in.
- They don't know how to move on to the other dimensions.

Ectoplasm

You see ghosts because of ectoplasm. Ectoplasm is a mist-like substance that is not completely solid, but is physical enough to be photographed. Some ghosts can be seen in colour although most are white.

How ghosts contact you

Ghosts communicate telepathically through thoughts. Unlike poltergeists, they do not wish to scare you. When ghosts appear, more than one person may see them, or only those sensitive to paranormal phenomena. Animals are very sensitive to the presence of a ghost because they are more attuned to higher frequencies.

Ways in which a ghost communicates

- He appears as a recognisable shape using ectoplasm (a white haze).
- He moves a photograph of himself when alive.
- He appears as a face in a mirror.
- His voice appears on a tape.
- A phone call is received and static and the deceased voice is heard faintly.
- You smell a flowery scent, or a perfume or tobacco connected to the person when alive.
- Electric lights are turned on and off.
- You feel a chill, tickle or touch to the back of your head or neck.

- You feel a cold breeze in part of the room when the rest of the room feels normal.
- You hear noises such as rapping, music or knocking, especially in the middle of the night.
- You feel there is someone else in the room.
- You wake and feel a weight pressing down on your chest.
- Machines keep breaking for no reason.
- A series of unexplained small fires happen.
- Small children say they can see someone else in the house.
- You pick up on negative emotions that don't seem to belong to you, for example, you get a feeling of fear or depression, especially around a certain room.

Famous ghosts

- The Tower of London: the two princes killed in 1483, Anne Boleyn, Guy Fawkes and Walter Raleigh.
- Raynham Hall, New York: the Brown Lady, first reported in 1835.
- Borley Rectory, Essex: various hauntings linked to its previous use as a Benedictine monastery.
- The Drury Lane Theatre, London. A ghost that reputedly is a young man killed in the 1700s.

History

Sightings of ghosts are universal to most cultures. The first recorded sighting was in 2000 BC in Babylonia. Ancient Rome also recorded many sightings of ghosts, including the phantom of Julius Caesar appearing to Brutus.

As well as homes, ghosts appear in places that have strong energetic associations – for example, places where many people have gathered, or where people have died – such as religious sites, theatres, pubs, castles, battlefields, cemeteries, sacred burial grounds and caves.

Sites of mass deaths, such as battlefields, particularly attract ghosts. When a number of people get killed at the same time, it is thought that souls can get trapped if there were not enough guides ready to open the portals between planes to guide them through to the next dimension. Some souls therefore carry on fighting on the astral plane, unaware the battle has ended. This is heard on the physical plane as sound phenomena.

Soul rescue

There are mediums who specialise in rescuing souls at this type of location. Only very experienced mediums should try this type of rescue. This is because the energy charge would be much too much for someone who is untrained.

What to do if you come across a ghost in your home

- First of all, remember that a ghost means you no harm. You are more powerful than it is. It is important to be free of any fear.
- Ask your spirit guide to stay with you.
- Surround yourself with white light.
- Light sage or a smudge stick. (These are available from New Age shops.) Blow out the flame and use the smoke to smudge the house. This will get rid of energy from negative emotions, though not the discarnate spirit.
- Talk to the spirit. Tell them the current date. Tell them that they cannot stay here. They are not welcome here as they do not belong here, but need now to go to the light.
- Ask your spirit guide to help them move to the light. Move from room to room, repeating the process.
- When you feel the house is cleaned, seal the home with white light.

HEALING

A spiritual healer acts as a channel for universal white light or God-energy from the spirit world to the patient. The healer may use a helper guide who specialises in medical matters, or may simply ask for energy from the higher Universe. A healer is only a medium, in the true sense of the word; that's to say a bridge between the two worlds. If he closes down the channel he has no innate ability.

How healing works

A healer may lay his hands directly on the patient, or may hold his hands at a slight distance from the body, within the aura. By doing this, he can sense areas where energy is needed and the nature of the illness or complaint. Next he directs energy to the patient.

Since an illness that manifests itself in the body is often the result of an imbalance within other auras, psychic healing takes place on a mind, spirit and body level. The energy is directed to restore the balance at subtle levels.

Some healers will charge for this. Others will ask for a donation or energy exchange. Some will give their time free of charge.

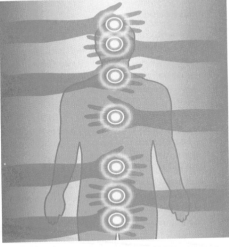

Healing hands

What you experience during healing

When the healer 'lays on' his hands, the patient may feel a change in temperature: hot or cold, or a tingling sensation. The release of inner tensions and blocks may leave him relaxed or energised afterwards.

The patient does not have to believe in healing or any spiritual or psychic powers to receive benefits.

Famous Healers

Harry Edwards (1893–1976) is one of the most famous recent healers. Although he did not become a healer until he was in his forties, he worked with many hundreds of patients in his healing centre, the Sanctuary. There are many stories of the cures he facilitated.

Edgar Cayce (1877–1945), the most famous healer of the first half of the twentieth century, was born in America. He became known as the 'sleeping prophet' because he appeared to sleep through his sessions as he channelled spirits. Cayce carried out more than 14,000 readings over 40 years. He made many predictions, notably about the end of the world. He also claimed to have information relating to the lost civilisation of Atlantis, the Pyramid of Giza and the Land of Mu.

Matthew Manning (1955–) is a famous modern English healer who came to prominence in the 1970s. He wrote several books about his experiences communicating with spirits after attracting poltergeist phenomena in the house in which he lived when a child. He now specialises in healing work and holds public seminars.

THOUGHT FORMS

A thought form is an energy shape that exists within the astro-mental field. A thought form exists as a result of an intense or persistent thought, belief or emotion.

Many thought forms cause disruptions in the emotions, mind or body. What a psychiatrist observes as a negative thought pattern in the subconscious, a psychic senses through the third eye as a parasite-like shape attached to the aura. These thought forms interfere with the balance of the aura and can produce physical ailments or distortions in emotions. They function like a fog that clouds the psyche.

They can originate either from the person themselves, or attach to the auras of sensitive people and children. Thought forms interfere with clarity of vision and can cause rigidity of thinking. Strong thought forms can induce mental illness or paranoia. Other signs of thought forms controlling a person's energy field are depression, addiction, a fixation on negative memories, phobias or anxiety.

Some people may carry thought forms that are also shared with a family group or occur within a particular culture. They have originated from intense shared emotions and beliefs and are known as a group mind.

HEALING YOURSELF

You may see a pain or discomfort that a person is experiencing as dark, stagnant energy patches in the aura or as a larger cloudlike mass. A thought form may be observed as foggy shapes or as a floating or static shape. Strong thought forms can look like dark energy channels extending with tentacles through the chakras and energy channels of the aura into the physical body and into the organs.

You may also feel changes in heat, weight, magnetism, vibration or energy or you may experience a tingling feeling in your hands. Some energy feels like mucus, with a heavy sticky quality.

You will gradually be able to recognise the correspondence between what you sense visually or kinesthetically and what that means in terms of diagnosis.

Basic body visualisation

Become proficient at seeing your own body in your mind's eye. It will allow you to notice with your psychic perception if any energy blocks are present and if there are any signs of physical illness in the body.

Through becoming familiar with your own body, you will also become more competent at scanning other people's bodies.

Visualisation exercise

1 Sit quietly, close your eyes, take a few deep breaths and go to your alpha state.

2 In your mind's eye, see your own body as a three dimensional image.

3 Study the exterior of your body from the front. Look first at the head, then the torso, then down to the feet.

4 Turn the body round and look at the back. What do you notice about how your body looks? Are there any physical markers such as wrinkles or moles? What does your hair look like? Your skin? Notice your height and weight. How would you describe what you see?

5 Open your eyes.

Now you are ready to practise two exercises where you will become more aware of how to test for imbalances and illnesses in your body. It will help you if you have studied a picture of the anatomy first so that you are aware of the major organs, the skeletal structure, the muscles, blood vessels and brain.

Self scanning exercise

1 Sit quietly, close your eyes, take a few deep breaths and go to your alpha state.

2 In your mind's eye, see your own body. Be aware of the exterior of your body from the top of your head down to your toes.

3 Imagine that you can enter into your body through your head.

4 Go into the bones and feel what they feel like.

5 Enter into the flesh and feel what it feels like.

6 Be aware of your blood vessels and your blood flowing. Feel what it feels like.

7 Enter each organ of your body.

8 Notice sensation such as colour, weight, temperature, movement and sound.

9 Pay attention to your instincts. Are there any imbalances or abnormalities in any part of your body? Try to pick up on these in any form or symbol you are given. You must rely on your intuition in this regard.

10 Leave your body.

11 Come back to the present and open your eyes.

Alternative self-scanning exercise

1 Sit quietly, close your eyes, take a few deep breaths and go to your alpha state.

2 Imagine you are enclosed in white light.

3 Bring into your awareness a gold disc and place it above your head. Notice the qualities of the disc. Is it bright and shiny or dull or scratched? If there are any blemishes on the disc it is an indication from your higher self that something needs balancing.

4 Next scan your chakras. Place your hands at each chakra point. See if you get a visual image or feel any imbalances.

5 Finally, run your hands down your body a few inches away from your physical body. Are there any places where you want to stop? Do you feel any changes in sensation or temperature?

6 Ask what these mean. See what answer floats up into your consciousness.

CLEARING YOUR ENERGY FIELD

Make sure you always protect yourself with white light from picking up other people's energies when you practise healing. If you have picked up energy in your energy field, you might experience:

- Low-level pains and aches.
- Feeling as if you are about to start a cold.
- Feeling sluggish, irritable, depressed or tired.
- Feel heavy or toxic.

How to clear your energy field

Smudging: use a ready-made smudge stick, sage or cedar. Light it, blow the flame out and simply waft the smoke around your body. This will clear the stagnant energy away.

Clear quartz crystals: hold the crystal in one hand. Ask the energy to move from your auric field into the crystal. Then clean the crystal in water containing half a teaspoon of sea salt. Or put the crystal outside in the sunlight and moonlight for 24 hours.

Baths: put half a cup of baking soda and about half a kilogramme of sea salt into a bathful of water. This will absorb the negative energy. After 15 minutes or so you will feel very refreshed. Or make tea from dried basil and put it in the bath water and soak in it for twenty minutes. Or add Epsom salts to your bath for the same effect.

HEALING OTHERS

Warning

Remember that you are not a doctor. Always advise a person to see a doctor if they are ill.

Checking the health of the chakras

A patient's chakras may be unde- or over-active. If a chakra is under active it may not be receiving enough energy flow from another linked chakra. If it is over-active, there may be a block in the outflow from the chakra to other chakras.

Diagnosis

You can use your hand as a scanner to become aware of the energies and to heal the body. Scan down the line of the chakras with your hands a short distance from the body. Use your intuition to feel blockages in a chakra. Your hand may want to stop at the chakra where there is a problem or you may feel a change in temperature or tingling.

Next, take note of the physical or psychological symptoms in a patient and link them to the correlation chart on the previous pages.

Brushing the auras away exercise

If you sense that there is general negative energy in

Name of chakra	Over-active
First chakra – root	Sluggishness, overweight, greed, materialism
Second chakra – sacral	Poor boundaries, excessive emotion, sex addiction, obsession
Third chakra – solar plexus	Aggression, blame, unfocused energy, over-activity
Fourth chakra – heart	Codependence, jealousy, poor boundaries
Fifth chakra – throat	Talking too much, inability to listen
Sixth chakra – third eye	Delusions, hallucinations, inability to concentrate, lying
Seventh chakra – crown	Dissociation, over-intellectualising, spiritual addiction

Under-active	Physical correspondence
Underweight, fear, lack of discipline	Adrenal glands, kidneys, legs, gonads, teeth, large intestine
Guilt, impotence, fear of enjoyment and emotion, frigidity	Reproductive system, circulation, kidneys, bladder
Shame, poor self esteem, passivity, fear, weak will	Stomach, adrenal glands, small intestine, pancreas, liver, digestion, spleen
Grief, criticism, loneliness, shyness, isolation, lack of empathy	Thymus gland, heart, immune system, blood, endocrine system, circulatory system
Fear of speaking out, inability to express self	Thyroid gland, lungs, vocal chords, mouth, neck
Poor memory, denial	Pineal or pituitary gland, eyes, ears, brain
Apathy, spiritual disconnection, materialism	Pineal or pituitary gland, brain, body, psyche

another person's aura, you can brush it away.

1 Ask the other person to close their eyes.

2 With the other person standing in front of you, go to your alpha state. Make sure you are surrounded by white light.

3 Imagine that you can grow your fingers as if there is a skeletal finger made of energy growing about 15 cm out of your physical finger.

4 Now hold your hands out with the fingers extended so that you are reaching into the aura of the other person. With your psychic fingers, brush downwards in big brush strokes like a giant hairbrush. Each stroke should reach from the top of the person's head right down to the bottom of their body. Brush all around the body.

5 Catch the stagnant energy in the strokes and bring it right down into the ground so it becomes part of the earth where it can transform into positive energy.

Correcting imbalances in yourself

Direct healing energy through your hands. See white light entering in through your crown and heart and flowing down through your hands.

Visualise correcting any imbalances in the body that you find. For example, if you are shown a picture of a bloated organ, you can visualise it deflating to its normal size. Or you might visualise your immune system fighting an infection inside your body. Any corrections should take place at the alpha level. As you use your psychic creativity and intuition to heal, state firmly to yourself 'I am now completely healthy in my body'.

Balancing the chakras exercise

Crystals, oils, incense and herbs corresponding to each chakra can be used to balance them.

Ask your spirit guides for help. Visualise the person's body in your mind's eye. Go to your alpha state and become aware of any imbalances. Make corrections as you are guided. Give the patient appropriate crystals or essences.

Healing relationships

Each time we come into interaction with another person an energy cord connects us through the chakras. The stronger the relationship the tougher the cord. Unless you cut the cord of unhealthy old relationships, you will continue to carry the energetic connection around with you.

Clairvoyants can see cords. In healthy relationships these cords glow with energy of white light or vibrant colours. In unhealthy relationships, the cords

Name of chakra	Crystal/gemstone	Oil/incense
First chakra – root	Obsidian, hematite, red jasper, bloodstone, ruby, garnet	Cedar
Second chakra – sacral	Coral, agate, carnelian	Gardenia
Third chakra – solar plexus	Tiger's eye, amber, citrine	Carnation
Fourth chakra – heart	Emerald, rose quartz, tourmaline	Lavender
Fifth chakra – throat	Turquoise, green aventurine, lapis lazuli	Frankincense
Sixth chakra – third eye	Quartz, blue sapphire, lapis Lazuli, sodalite	Star anise
Seventh chakra – crown	Diamond, moonstone, white opal, amethyst	Lotus

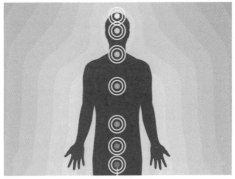

Balancing the chakras

can look diseased, dark, dull, or rigid. In a codependent relationship, the chord becomes like a sticky tentacle or hook reaching out from the needy person to the other.

Healers can reach psychically within the body and pull out unhealthy chords, or clean them with cosmic white light energy. If appropriate they can reconnect them.

Cutting cords

- You can cut your own cords between you and another person by directing white love energy from the cosmic source through your heart to the other person.

- Surround each of you with white light and gently cut the chord with a sword of white light or pull the chord out gently.
- Practise this regularly and you will feel lighter and happier as a person. You will also feel your relationships improve. This will only work if you are genuinely able to feel love and forgiveness for the other person.

Absent healing

The patient does not need to be present for healing to take place. With a name or a photograph, healing can be directed from the healer to a patient at any distance. Spiritualist churches and psychic groups often have a list where you can add the name of anyone who needs healing. The intention of the healer directs the healing energy to the place where it is needed. The spirit guides who are in charge of healing will act according to the intention of the psychics.

Reiki

Reiki is a popular healing technique that originated in Japan. It is said to have been discovered through a vision by Dr Mikao Usui in the 1800s, and was bought to the West by Mrs Hawayo Takeo. Dr Usui channelled a number of symbols that allowed him to tap into the universal life force. The word reiki comes from the

Japanese 'rei' meaning 'spirit' and 'ki' – meaning 'life force' – the Japanese equivalent of the Chinese 'chi'.

Reiki taps into universal energy to treat the whole person: the mind, body, emotions and spirit. Reiki practitioners are initiated into the energies of reiki by a reiki master. Reiki is not dependent on an individual's level of spiritual or psychic development. It uses six specific hand positions on a person's body to undo blocks that cause pain or illness and allow the life force to flow freely once more.

Reiki

USING TOOLS FOR HEALING

Dowsing technique

1 To diagnose an under- or over-active chakra, you can use a dowsing rod. This can be made simply from a metal coat hanger, by cutting and bending it so that it is a straight piece of rod. Next bend it to a 90-degree angle.

2 Hold the rod in your right hand pointing towards the person you are diagnosing. They may stand or sit. Use your left hand to scan the person you are diagnosing with your left hand. Hold your hand at the level of the aura.

3 Ask the dowsing rod to swing one way to indicate a blockage in the chakra caused by under-active functioning and in the opposite direction to indicate over-activity. Make a note of which chakras need adjustment.

Pendulum technique

You can use a pendulum in the same way directly over or in front of the person you are diagnosing. Check each chakra in turn.

PSYCHIC SURGERY

Psychic surgery is a phenomena mainly associated with the Philippines and Brazil. Psychic surgeons claim to extract objects such as tumours from the body. The theory is that the surgeon raises the vibration of their physical hand so that it can pass through tissue without the use of antibiotics.

However, many psychic surgeons have been exposed as frauds using sleight-of-hand and animal blood.

History

Psychic surgery started in the 1940s in the Philippines with Eleuterio Terte, who trained many students and was associated with an organisation called the Union Espiritista Christiana de Filipinas.

In Brazil, many psychic doctors in the 1950s were associated with a spiritualist religion called Kardecism. Jose Arigo was a psychic surgeon who was born in Brazil at the beginning of the last century and died in 1971. He became a healer after saving the life of a relative who was dying of an illness with no known cause. As the woman lay dying, Jose took a kitchen knife and immediately used it to remove a huge tumour. Jose treated many people using a spirit guide called Adolphus Fritz. However, he was twice imprisoned in the 1950s and '60s for practising medicine illegally.

PSYCHIC RESEARCH

How do you know whether someone is psychic, a fraud or just crazy? Fraudulant mediums have been common since the 1800s. While well-known modern day mediums and psychics appear to be sincere in what they are doing, how do they prove that they have genuine powers?

In the last century, a great number of experiments were carried out to see whether or not psychic powers were real. Parapsychology is the current study of phenomena such as telepathy and clairvoyance. It sets out to examine whether the mind can influence physical phenomena.

Sceptics do not believe sufficient evidence exists for the existence of extrasensory powers (ESP) and some refer to parapsychology as a pseudoscience. But counter to this, many well-known scientists have considered the field worthy of examination. These include:

- Austrian theoretical physicist Wolfgang Pauli
- Brian Josephson, who won the Nobel Prize in Physics in 1973
- Susan Blackmore, author of the Meme Machine
- English chemist and physicist William Crookes
- American astronaut Edgar Mitchell
- Physicist Harold E Puthoff

- Chemist and philosopher Carl Reichenbach
- Joseph B Rhine, the founder of the Journal of Parapsychology

Research institutes

There are a number of research institutes and laboratories throughout the world that currently carry out research into psychic powers. These include:

- Koestler Parapsychology Unit, University of Edinburgh, Scotland
- Rhine Research Center, North Carolina
- Perrot-Warrick Research Unit, University of Hertfordshire, England
- PEAR Laboratory, Princeton University, New Jersey
- Eötvös Loránd University of Budapest, Hungary
- Cognitive Sciences Laboratory, Pao Alto, California
- University of Amsterdam, Netherlands
- Insitut für Grenzgebiete der Psychologie und Psychohygiene, Frieburg, Germany

Experiments

There are three main types of experments that have been used to detect psychic powers:

Remote viewing experiments

Remote viewing was developed as one of the main ways in which parapsychologists could examine clairvoyance in a controlled environment. In remote viewing experiments, the viewer is asked to give information about a person or object that is hidden from their sight.

The first experiment was first developed by Russell Targ and Harold Puthoff in 1972 during the Cold War at the Stanford Research Institute in California on behalf of the CIA. The experiments were known as the Stargate program and were only acknowledged to have existed in 1995. The experiments apparently were begun after it was discovered that the Soviet Union had already spent over 60 million roubles on psychic research in the 1970s.

Gansfield experiments

Gansfield is a German word meaning 'whole field.' In a Gansfield experiment, a subject is put in an environment where external sensory distractions such as light and sound are excluded, to keep the mind clear. The subject is asked to receive images telepathically from a sender. The subject describes the impressions they receive. At the end of the session, the subject is shown a number of images and he must choose the one he thinks is the one that was being thought about by the sender.

On average, Gansfield experiments achieve results that are slightly better than could be statistically achieved by chance (about 34% versus 25%).

Random number generator (RNG) experiments

A random number generator is a machine that throws up a series of ones and zeros in a random fashion. The subject of the experiment is asked to focus on changing the sequence of the numbers so that they become less random, thereby showing evidence of psychokinesis (telekinesis).

Research has found that consistent focus by subjects does, in fact, produce higher occurrences of one particular number. The machine is controlled by computer to avoid the possibility of human interference. The conclusion from the experiments so far would appear to be that mind can indeed influence matter.

Near-Death experiences (NDEs)

Also of great interest to researchers are near-death experiences (NDEs) because they appear to provide us with evidence of the existence of the invisible Universe and other planes. These experiences take place when a person returns from the brink of death even after he may have been declared dead for several minutes. Studies of individuals who have had near-death experiences show many similarities in their accounts, regardless of their age, culture or religious beliefs.

A near-death experience is often precipitated by a sudden trauma such as a heart attack or a crisis during a surgical procedure. The person has an immediate feeling that they are separating from their physical body, rising up into the air, so that they can look down and be aware of what is happening around the body they are leaving. This is experienced as a peaceful calm process, even though there may be a flurry of activity going on around their physical body. Sometimes the person can describe exactly what was happening during this crisis point when they return to life, for example, they might see a doctor trying to jolt them back to life or hear a snatch of a conversation.

The person then sees a dark tunnel through which they begin to float. At the end of the tunnel is a white light that draws them down it. Friends and family who have already passed over to the other side are waiting to greet them beyond the white light. Some people feel a sense of fear, but most describe feeling pure love filling them.

It is thought that the tunnel represents a portal from the physical to the spirit planes. The white light is astral light, otherwise known as God's light or universal light.

Most recently, scientists have suggested that near-death experiences may be caused by a portion of the brain misfiring under stress or by the activation of certain brain regions that are also active during the dream state.

Proof of psychic ability

Proving or disproving psychic abililty is controversial. In 1924, the Scientific American Magazine offered a financial prize to anyone who could produce a 'visible psychic manifestation'. A medium called 'Marjory' Mina Crandon claimed the reward. But the panel from the magazine failed to agree whether her powers were genuine and, without further proof, did not award the prize.

A prize was also offered in the 1900s to any magician who could replicate the table-lifting feats of the well-known medium of the time, Eusapia Palladino. None came forth, but in 1910, Eusapia admitted that she had used trickery to produce the phenomena. This continued to feed the scepticism of those who disputed the claims of those who claimed to be in contact with the dead.

Many modern magicians use trickery to display abilities that seem to mimic psychic phenomena. James Randi is one of the foremost modern critics of the paranormal. He was a professional magician who gained fame in 1972 when he challenged Uri Geller to prove his abilities. He was one of the founding members of the Committee for Scientific Investigation of Claims of the Paranormal and is committed to exposing frauds in the psychic industry. In 1987 he wrote an exposé on the evangelist and faith healer Peter Poppoff. He has offered a prize of US$1 million to anyone who can demonstrate supernatural powers under defined scientific testing criteria.

James Randi carried out the famous Project Alpha hoax, which involved two fake psychics and amateur magicains, Steve Shaw and Michael Edwards. Their abilities (including spoon-bending) were subjected to various tests at the McDonnell Laboratory for Psychical Research. The experiments appeared to prove that the two were psychic, but in fact their results were produced through trickery. The positive results of the experiments were not exposed as fakes until some time later, but the exposure may have discouraged other prospective experimenters.

The Committee for the Scientific Investigation of Claims of the Paranormal (CSICOP), a group of professional (stage) magicians and scientists and others, is one of the foremost groups continuing to put forward the anti-paranormal case. The Skeptics Society similarly puts forward its point of view on what it classifies as irrational beliefs or pseudoscience.

FURTHER READING AND INFORMATION

Books

Abadie, MJ. *Your Psychic Potential* (Adams Media Corp. 1995)

Berkowitz, Rita and Deborah S. Romaine. *Empowering your Life with Angels.* (Alpha Books 2003)

Cayce, Edgar. *You Can Remember Your Past Lives* (Warner, 1989)

Choquette, Sonia. *Balancing your Chakras,* (Piatkus, 2000)

Choquette, Sonia. *Your Heart's Desire: Instructions for Creating the Life You Really Want.* (Three Rivers Press, 1997)

Dossey, Larry. *Healing Words: the Power of Prayer and the Practice of Medicine* (Harper San Francisco, 1997)

Eason, Cassandra. *Contact your Spirit Guides* (Quantum, 2005)

Edward, John. *After Life: Answers from the Other Side* (Hayhouse, 2003)

Cayce, Edgar. *You Can Remember your Past Lives* (Warner, 1989)

Courtney, Hazel. *The Evidence for the Sixth Sense* (Cico, 2005)

Finkelstein, Arthur. *Your Past Lives and the Healing Process* (50 Gates Publishing Company, 1997)

Fortune, Dion. *Psychic Self-Defence* (The Aquarian Press, 1988)

Foster Case, Paul. *The Tarot* (Builders of the Adytum, 1990)

Hall, Judy. *The Way of Psychic Protection* (Thorsons, 2001)

Hay, Louise. *Heal Your Body* (Hay House, 1993)

Hill, Dawn. *Edge of Reality* (Pan Books, 1990)

Ingerman, Sandra. *Soul Retrieval: Mending the Fragmented Self* (Harper San Francisco, 1991)

Kahili King, Serge. *Urban Shaman* (Simon & Schuster, 1990)

LaBerge, Stephen. *Exploring the World of Lucid Dreaming* (Ballantine, 1991)

Lewis, James R. *The Dream Encyclopedia* (Visible Ink Press, 1995)

Mickaharic, Draja. *Spiritual Cleansing* (Samuel Weiser, 1982)

Montgomery, Ruth. *A World Beyond* (Fawcett Crest, 1991)

Moody, Raymond Jr. *Life after Life* (Harper San Francisco 2001)

Moore, Thomas. *Care of the Soul* (HarperCollins, 1994)

Pearsall, Reginald. *The Table Rappers* (Sutton, 2004)

Rand, William. *Reiki, The Healing Touch* (Vision Publications, 2000)

Roman, Sanaya, and Duane Packer. *Opening to Channel: How to Connect With Your Guide.* (HJ Kramer, 1987)

Sutphen, Dick. *Unseen Influences* (Pocket Books, 1982)

Stein, Diane. *Essential Reiki: A Complete Guide to an Ancient Healing Art* (Crossing Press, 1995)

Stuart, Rowenna. *Gem Tarot* (Collins, 1998) *Gem Palm Reading* (Collins, 2000)

Radin, Dean. *The Conscious Universe* (HarperCollins, 1997)

Bellof, John. *Parapsychology: A Concise History* (St Martin's Press, 1993)

Weiss, Brian. *Many Lives, Many Masters* (Simon & Schuster, 1988)

Weiss, Brian. *Through Time Into Healing* (Simon & Schuster, 1992)

Research and other organisations

Society for Psychical Research (SPR). The original scientific society founded in London in 1882.
http://www.spr.ac.uk

American Society for Psychical Research (ASPR).
http://www.aspr.com

Spirit Release Foundation.
http: //www.spiritrelease.com

National Federation of Spiritual Healers.
http://www.nfsh.org.uk

College of Psychic Studies London.
http://www.collegeof psychicstudies.co.uk

Spiritualist Association of Great Britain (SAGB).
http://www.sagb.org.uk

World Federation of Healing (WFH).
http://www.wfh.org.uk

International Association for Near-Death Studies.
http://www.iands.org

Institute for Parapsychology (Rhine Research Centre).
http://www.rhine.org

National Guild of Hypnotists USA.
http://www.ngh.net

Parapsychology Association, New York.
http:// www.parapsychology.org

Barbara Brennan School of Healing.
http:// www.barbarabrennan.com

Sceptics

The Skeptics Society.
http://www.skeptic.com

The Committee for the Scientific Investigation of Claims of the Paranormal.
http://www.csicop.org

INDEX

192

Index